D1686422
9780804463430

MICHELE CASCELLA

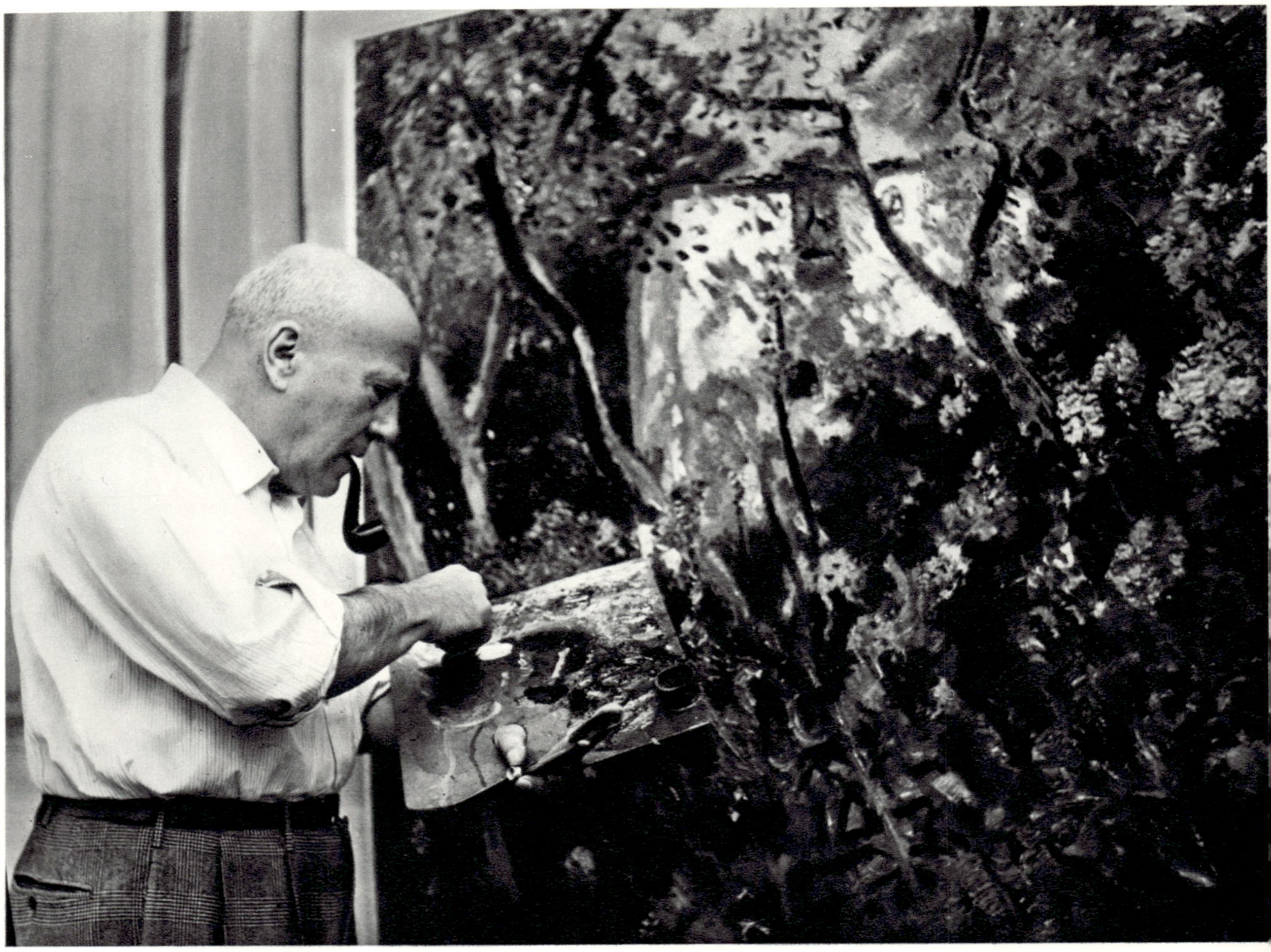

MICHELE CASCELLA

TEXT BY
JEHANNE SALINGER

FREDERICK UNGAR PUBLISHING CO.
NEW YORK

Copyright © 1965 by Michele Cascella

Library of Congress Catalog Card No. 65-19173

Printed in Italy

MICHELE CASCELLA

was born in Ortona a Mare September 7, 1892. He began his artistic career as a young man under the guidance of his father, Basilio. Through the hard work of apprenticeship, Michele learned the most varied techniques, from lithography and oil painting to crayon and watercolor.

The first Cascella exhibit was held at the Famiglia Artistica in Milan, together with works by his brother Tommaso. Then followed exhibits in Paris in 1909 and 1910, the latter held at the Salon d'Automne.

The First World War found him a soldier at the front where, thanks to the interest of General Enrico Caviglia, he was permitted to paint and draw life on the battlefields as it was.

In 1919 he went to Milan, where he was received by the poet Clemente Rebora, with whom he shared the first years after the war. In 1928 he exhibited in Brussels, 1929 in London, 1931 again in Paris; 1937 in Johannesburg, 1948 in Buenos Aires, and from 1959 on in some of the outstanding communities in the United States. His works were shown at the Biennale of Venice from 1928 through 1942. They have also been presented at some of the most important national and international exhibits.

Cascella's main interest is oil painting; he also devoted long periods to scenic design and ceramics.

In 1955 his native city of Ortona a Mare honored Cascella and his brothers Tommaso and Gioacchino and presented Michele Cascella with a gold medal.

Cascella's works can be found in some of the foremost public and private art collections. The artist divides his time among Portofino, Milan, Paris and the United States.

JEHANNE SALINGER

has been a writer and lecturer on art for thirty years in Canada and on the West Coast. She published the first magazine on art ever to come out of California. (It was later merged with the late Peyton Boswell's ART DIGEST.*)*

Mrs. Salinger has been art critic for several major daily newspapers in San Francisco, and also writes frequently for art publications and other periodicals. Born and educated in France, she has a wide frame of reference in the field of art, knowing many of the leading artists of our time. She makes her home in Carmel-by-the-Sea, California, and in private life is Mrs. Jerome Carlson.

The Poetess, 1914

6 ¾ x 8 inches

ment have their acrobats as did earlier fashions—these latecomers are creating a crisis of a sort. The "old guard" of the nonfigurative factions are dismayed at what they consider foul play. Museum directors and art dealers are trapped. A new trend threatens to inundate them just after their successful indoctrination of the general public and their own clients. Faced with a semblance of figurative formulation, as in the case of the New Realists and the farcical Pop Art entertainers, they are trying to disentangle them-

11

Fatigue Shoes, 1915   6 ¾ x 8 inches

selves. The fact is that the major part of these art acrobatics has so destroyed art standards that a devaluation of their product is at hand—a sad ending for many an investor in false values.

With a painter such as Cascella we are in the company of one who has traditions and who has disciplined himself, since early youth, in good old-fashioned draughtsmanship and in hard work. I have had a chance to see him frequently in his California studio, near the campus of Stanford University at Palo Alto, where he is in constant renewal.

Born in the Abruzzi, near the Adriatic Sea, in 1892, the artist was introduced to painting by his father, Basilio Cascella. Not satisfied with using one medium, he has explored the techniques of lithography, and has become a master in pastel and in watercolor.

Cascella was only fifteen when he held his first exhibition at "La Famiglia Artistica" in Milan. During the First World War, he was asked to record some of the episodes on the front lines. Within a few years he had successful exhibitions in Milan, where he has a home and studio, in Brussels, London, Paris, Buenos Aires, Geneva, Lausanne and in the United States.

In the thirties he moved to the Italian Riviera and took a studio on the gulf of Genoa in the charming port of Portofino. Cascella's studio, perched on the hillside, dominates the blue water of the Mediterranean Sea. He was known as the "King of Portofino." However, this insatiable artist is not to be identified, in a static manner, with any one place. He paints in Rome, in Milan, in Paris, in New York, in San Francisco, or along the cypress-haunted coast of the Monterey Peninsula in California. In any season, he is likely to linger along a street, anywhere—in Italy, in France, or in the United States—and to encompass so much of what he sees and perceives with his sensibility as an artist and as a human being that he will, at times, overrun his own cup, and then his canvas will be a synthesis of a whole moment of life, or of the mood of a city. This he accomplished in his rendition of Fisherman's Wharf in San Francisco, where he did not paint any part of the scene; rather, through a compact of architectural motives, a play of forms, space, and texture, in a sort of pictural shorthand, he transferred it all to his canvas — the crabs, the arches of the Golden Gate, the fishing boats.

He did something of the sort in his "Obsession of New York" (1961), blending mood and character elements with architectural notations. Greenwich Village is here, circuited, as it were, in a motif of figures in heteroclite apparel being harangued by a youth wearing tights; the romance of New York is here too, with the steeple of St. Patrick's Cathedral, the skyscraper apartment houses of Central Park reaching for heaven, and a fluttering of trees, with Cascella's palette at its most subtle.

One of Cascella's dominant traits is his ability to enter into the very flesh of his subject matter. His paintings of Portofino are variations on the soft sway of sails, yachts, and boats against the blue of the water and the blue of the sky, on the terraces of beach-side cafes gay with people, on the hillside houses in bright yellow with red tile roofs. This is the Cascella of the

The Cathedral of Aquileia, 1914.   Collection G. Cavazzini, Parma   17 ¾ x 27 ½ inches

Mediterranean climate. There is gaiety in these particular paintings, and they lead one to think of Dufy, although Cascella is more of a purist when it comes to the articulation of his line.

Watch him now, with his easel set along the gray Pacific in Carmel-by-the-Sea. The gnarled cypresses that have gained his attention are all at once solemn, architectural. There is no caressing light coming through their tangled branches; there is a misty veil of fog, all-enveloping. The outstretched roots call for a detailed drawing.

Sailboats in Ischia, 1915. Collection Cornelius V. Starr, New York   27 ½ x 39 ¼ inches

The actual shapes of the branches and the main trunk have a truth of their own. Between the branches the sand beach brings up a soft gray light from the ocean, and one feels the warmish fog upon the whole scene.

In his native Abruzzi, he paints veiled swamps like so many mirrors among trees — the tender green of the trees and the silvery tones of the water all conforming to the atmospheric light and to the mood of his motif. In American cities, he suddenly hardens and even comes to paint a

Irises (pastel), 1912   21 ¾ x 34 inches

pedestrian taxicab standing, in abeyance, in front of a suburban cottage.

A fine painter of landscapes, of street scenes, Cascella is also singled out as a portrait painter. Witness the portrait of his daughter or those two portraits, "The Red Jacket - 1918 (property of Liana Basedow)" and "An Old Sailor from Pescara." He will always be noted for his charcoal portrait of his Milan friend, "The Poet Clemente Rebora."

Cascella's many paintings of flowers, which

are dispersed around the world among collectors, represent another facet of his art. Sometimes it is a vast copper jug filled with wild flowers and a few garden flowers mixed in for the sake of diversity. With an eye sensitized to seductive forms and to color, and a sensitivity to tactile qualities, he never gets involved in minuteness. His paintings of flowers are seductive, and bear, in their very rendition, the imprint of Cascella.

It is not competence alone which makes an artist, nor is it just his intellect. When one has added all of the factors that enter into a good canvas—draughtsmanship, forms, color, a sense of pattern, of design—one has only indulged in an enumeration. The artist and his intuitive gift, that imponderable dimension that gives a painting its own reality, its own authenticity, aside and apart from the subject, bring all the other factors to life.

A few times in his long career, Cascella has reached to the great moment in art. Of these great moments, none, perhaps, in the entire work of this artist to date, is finer than his memorable canvas of the "Canonization of Andrea Uberto Fournet." Given the rare privilege of painting during the ceremonies at St. Peter's in 1933, he created here the most notable example of a painting in which come into play all the skills of a superb draughtsman with a rich palette, all the respect and understanding of the architectural detail, all the strength and power of the understatement. There is no mannerism of detail, yet he has not neglected the values presented by the ceiling, the arches, the columns of the Sacred Chapel, the nave crowded with pious attendants. In massing

The Red Jacket, 1918. Collection Mrs. Liana Basedow, Rome

his groupings, arranging his motifs as in a vast tapestry, he has created a canvas of superlative order. Were it the only painting left by Michele Cascella for succeeding generations to view, this artist from the Abruzzi, by the Adriatic Sea, would leave his mark indelibly.

He has brought to other canvases the same kind of skill in varying degrees of artistry, many times reaching to a very high level of excellence. I am thinking now of one cityscape, "New York Sixth Avenue," painted in 1962, a concerto in blue, gray, and brown. I am also looking with my mind's eye at his Odilon Redon-like flower study in veiled white and soft yellows against a background of tender dove gray, titled "Flowers of California."

In a less formalized form he has painted in broad strokes, stated in bold colors, his impressions of a mesh of freeways in South San Francisco: trucks, buses, and automobiles in a continuous streamer of yellows and bluish reds, and, in the distance, houses and taller buildings in espalier against a cotton-strewn sky.

Competing with his own performances, Cascella also commands attention as a painter of trees. Whether he is attracted by the fabled cypresses of the Monterey Coast in California, or by the affluence of foliage on the edge of the woods in Italy, he has a loving devotion to trees. Witness that feast of gold and copper in the autumn trees around the Medici Fountain in the Luxembourg Gardens, in Paris, or the rythmic repetition of slender tree trunks in his painting of tree-lined alleys in the Tuileries, and we agree that his pictorial sense rarely misleads him. Watch how he

Harvest in the Abruzzi, 1923. Banca Nazionale del Lavoro, Rome   59 1/8 x 79 inches

CASCELLA AS A WATERCOLOR PAINTER

Known in Europe, South America, and the United States for his oil paintings, Michele Cascella deserves a place of his own for his work in watercolor. Artists of excellence who use this medium are proud to be found in his company.

Contrary to the general concept that water-

23

Russian Student, 1928   30 ¾ x 43 ¼ inches

color is a rapid method, a means to record, in a brief moment, one's impression or the depiction of a scene, Cascella works deliberately at watercolor, and his finest qualities as an artist are put to their maximum use here.

He works much as Rembrandt did. He executes a pen-and-ink drawing, then washes his colors in. Examine, if you will, the animals of Rembrandt—his rabbit, his owl, his insects—and study his underlay of pen and ink and the manner in which he applies his color. Cascella goes at it similarly — except that he likes landmarks, monuments, flowers—detailing meticulously the parts that appeal the most to his intellect and to his sensibilities. Watch how he washes over the drawing, here in broad light and shade massings, there indulging in atmospheric transparencies or clear, luminous effects.

His consummate skill as a draughtsman serves him well in paintings such as "Pont des Arts, Paris," or in his rendition of "La Fontana di Trevi, Roma (property of Miss Joyce Passetti)" or again in "The House of Keats and Shelley, Rome." One of his great watercolor paintings is "The Fountain of Trevi." The statues in the arches, the horses adorning the fountain, the water falling in cascades, every phase of this fine painting has been considered, studied, and handled with the utmost care, yet the total effect is one of a simple happening. It is there—effortless, easy, actual.

He paints flowers in a slightly more casual manner. In his aquarelles of flowers there is no fully realized pen-and-ink drawing under the washes, only notations that underscore values of form, give accents to this or that tonality.

Cascella has a brilliant palette and he is the master of that palette. He uses it at will, now in full regalia when inspired by light and a great deal of color, then again delicate or subdued.

CASCELLA AS A MAN AND AS AN ARTIST

This artist, now in the eighth decade of his life, paints without letup, with the vigor and the zest of a man of thirty. An early riser, he not uncommonly starts painting shortly after dawn, when the light is soft and clean and before the spell is broken by the day's activities. On the one hand he loves life and people, on the other he loves the silence of his studio. He goes to bed early and keeps himself fit so as to do justice to his work. An avid reader, he keeps abreast of world events, of political thoughts and trends, of scientific achievements. He is most sensitive to music, classical and light, and considers it the greatest single stimulant in his life. His interests are manifold, in fact, all-encompassing. He is in step with our day. His recent canvases stay with him for a while. He will not permit them to be seen until he is satisfied that he has reached his maximum potential in this or that particular painting. He can get rashly critical of his own work, and if he feels that one of his paintings has not come up to his concept, he will turn its face to the wall, brood over it, then hide it away for good, or even destroy it.

Like many artists of excellence, he will, on

Self Portrait, 1942.   Collection Dr. Delfo Palmerio, Turin

21 ¾ x 29 ½ inches

27

Artists at Montmartre, 1960. Collection Mr. and Mrs. Walter H. Shorenstein, San Francisco
24 x 36 1/8 inches

the other hand, rejoice over a very good canvas and point out to visitors in his studio all of its fine points, discussing it as though someone else had painted it. All of these traits belong to a man who has a great gusto for life. A fine host, he is, however, very selective in his associations, and will not be assailed by empty adulation or fatuous words. He can be warm and he can be aloof and totally inexpressive

As strange as it may seem to some, this Italian of old lineage, the scion of a family of artists, who

The Artist's Daughter, 1949. Collection Cornelius V. Starr, New York 27 ½ x 39 ¼ inches

The House of Keats and Shelley, Rome, 1959.   Collection Carlo Ermoli, Milan   28 ¾ x 49 inches

returns frequently to his homeland, has become fascinated with the United States. He loves California, where he maintains a permanent studio, in addition to his studios in Milan and Portofino, and he has entered into the mood of the American city, of the California landscape, in a way that is quite uncommon among artists who have come from other parts of the world. He marvels at the crisscrossing of freeways, with their loops interlaced in an amazing jigsaw. He views them with a childlike sense of awe. The never-ending chain of motorcars have for him a magnetic attraction. His canvases are poems proclaiming the significance of the expanding vistas of America. His sense of wonder at the typically American object will, on occasion, reveal itself in such details as a pack of cigarettes, placed on the corner of a table which he has used to set one of his memorable vases of flowers, on which he will have written minutely: "Lucky Strike."

However, with all his involvement in the American scene, there are times when nostalgia is present. Witness some of his still lifes painted in his California studio, set against a background of patches of blue Mediterranean water with lazy boats at anchor. There are days when his blue eyes will suddenly look far away as he pours a glass of Punt e Mes for a friend. Cascella's sensitivity to his American environment, his need to return to his homeland every so often, bespeak a man true to himself, true to his art as well.

Neither a follower nor an innovator, Michele Cascella stands on his own: a painter who belongs to no school, follows no formula, but who, when he reaches his maximum, has a quality that sets him apart from the maelstrom.

When the procession of the many schools of painting has finally passed across the art stage, when the experimenters who mistake the means for the end have come to the final impasse, Michele Cascella, whose acceptance by art lovers and art connoisseurs has not waited for the outcome of the battle of the "isms," will assume his full

Piazza Santa Maria Novella, Florence, 1949. Museum of Modern Art, Paris

stature. After the day of awakening, museum directors and critics alike will find it refreshing to contemplate the work of artists who have remained conscious of traditions, sensitive to their environment, true to nature, and true to their own response; artists considerate of skills and of disciplines, and aware of life. Michele Cascella is such an artist.

BIBLIOGRAPHY
arranged chronologically

CARLO CARRÁ: *Michele Cascella.* Monograph with reproductions in black and white. Edizione d'arte Castagneri, Milan, 1925

VINCENZO COSTANTINI and GIOVANNI TITTA ROSA: *Michele Cascella.* Monograph with reproductions in black and white and in color. Edizioni d'Arte Gea, Milan, 1925

VINCENZO BUCCI: Catalogue introduction, exhibit at *Galleria Pesaro di Milano*, Milan, 1925

UGO NEBBIA: *La XV Esposizione internazionale di Venezia.* Istituto d'Arti grafiche Editore, Bergamo, 1926

ARSÈNE ALEXANDRE: Catalogue introduction, exhibit at *Gallery 23*, Paris, January 1931

ARSÈNE ALEXANDRE: "Michele Cascella." *Le Figaro*, Paris, January 17, 1931

VINCENZO BUCCI: "Michele Cascella." *Il Corriere della Sera*, Milan, February 28, 1932

FRANÇOIS SOLLAR: "Michele Cascella." *Art et Décoration*, Paris, August 1932

CAMILLE MAUCLAIRE: Catalogue introduction, exhibit at *Gallery Bernheim Jeune of Paris*, Paris, 1932

VINCENZO COSTANTINI: *Pittura contemporanea italiana.* Ulrico Hoepli Editore, Milan, 1934

RENÉ SHAPESHAK: Catalogue introduction, exhibit at *Johannesburg*, Johannesburg, 1937

VINCENZO COSTANTINI: *Maioliche di Michele Cascella.* Edizioni della Galleria Pesaro, Milan, 1938

G. B. ANGIOLETTI: *Michele Cascella.* Monograph with reproductions in black and white and in color. Ulrico Hoepli Editore, Milan, 1940

GIOVANNI TITTA ROSA: Catalogue introduction, exhibit at *Galleria Dedalo di Milano*, Milan, November, 1945

MARZIANO BERNARDI: "Cascella e Tomea." Various pieces of criticism, *Gazzetta del Popolo*, Turin, February 15, 1946

ARRIGO ANGIOLINI: "Pittori che espongono: Michele Cascella." *Il Lavoro Nuovo*, Genoa, June 18, 1946

GIORGIO DE CHIRICO: Catalogue introduction, exhibit at *"The Mid 20th Gallery,"* Los Angeles, 1948

ORIO VERGANI: *Paesaggi parigini di M. Cascella.* Edizione di Piero Fornasetti, Milan, 1949.

BARNETT D. CONLAN: "Cascella's Italian Painting." *Daily Mail*, London, May, 1949

GABRIEL FAURE: Catalogue introduction, exhibit at *Gallery Allard*, Paris, May, 1949

RENÉ DOMERGUE: "M. Cascella." *L'Aube*, Paris, June 8, 1949

LORENZO BOCCHI: "Miguel Cascella en la cuidad luz." *Histonium*, Buenos Aires, August, 1949

GIORGIO NICODEMI: *La quadreria della Edison.* Edizione "L'Arte," Milan, 1949

—: *Italy today.* "Italian Contemporaries." Editorial and Business Office, New York, 1951

V. GUZZI: "Le mostre d'arte: Savelli e Cascella." *Il Tempo*, Rome, June 6, 1951

The Artist's Studio, 1958   31 ⅞ x 39 ¼ inches

CESARE GHIGLIONE: "Note d'arte." *Il Secolo XIX*, Genoa, June 17, 1951

ARRIGO ANGIOLINI: "Finestra sull'arte: I paesaggi di Michele Cascella sono una vivida orchestrazione di tutti i colori di Portofino." *Il Lavoro Nuovo*, Genoa, June 21, 1951

GIOVANNI DESCALZO: "Un teatro inimitabile: La piazzetta di Portofino." *Il Giornale*, Naples, August 31, 1951

GIOVANNI TITTA ROSA: "Incontro con il pittore Cascella." *La Nuova Stampa*, Turin, September 15, 1951

GUIDO GUIDA: "Un maestro della pittura italiana contemporanea." *La Via*, Rome, September 22, 1951

SALVATOR GOTTA: "Michele Cascella a Portofino." *Il Nuovo Corriere d'Informazione*, Milan, May 20-21, 1952

LEONARDO BORGESE: Introduction to the exhibit of *Michele Cascella*. Artistic prints by Richard Ginori Company, Milan, 1953

RAFFAELE CARRIERI: "Elegiaco Cascella." *Epoca*, Milan, January 17, 1953

VINCENZO COSTANTINI: "Un pittore sempre moderno: Michele Cascella." *Corriere Lombardo*, Milan, January 21, 1953

Trinitá dei Monti, Rome, 1959.   Collection Fred Zinnemann, Hollywood, California   29 ½ x 51 ⅛ inches

Leonardo Borgese: "Michele Cascella." *Il Nuovo Corriere della Sera*, Milan, January 22, 1953

Mario Radice: "Michele Cascella." *L'Italia*, Milan, January 23, 1953

Agnoldomenico Pica: "Carriera di un pittore." *La Patria*, Milan, January 31, 1953

Anita Pensotti: "L'abruzzese Cascella." *Oggi*, Milan, February 2, 1953

Piero Scarpa: "Mostre d'arte: Michele Cascella." *Il Messaggero*, Rome, May 9, 1953

Vincenzo Costantini: "Le opere e i sogni di Michele Cascella." *Corriere Lombardo*, Milan, July 15-16, 1953

Indro Montanelli: "Incontri: Michele Cascella." *Il Nuovo Corriere della Sera*, Milan, November 5, 1953

Marziano Bernardi: "Cascella a Lugano." *La Nuova Stampa*, Turin, July 27, 1954

G. C. Ghiglione: "Successo in Svizzera di un pittore sincero." *Il Secolo XIX*, Genoa, August 31, 1954

Orio Vergani: "Quadri di Cascella a Lugano." *Il Nuovo Corriere di Informazione*, Milan, September 1, 1954

Renzo Biasion: "Ha reso celebri alberi e barche di Portofino." *Oggi*, Milan, September 2, 1954

André Carpassity: "Avec Cascella, maître de la couleur." *Le Jour*, Beyrouth, September 28, 1954

—: "Significato del successo di un pittore italiano." *La Stampa Italiana*, Buenos Aires, October 14, 1954

Albert Rheinwarld: "Michel Cascella au Musée d'art." *Journal de Genève*, Geneva, October 22, 1954

—: "Il vero di Cascella." *Le Ore*, Rome, November 1954

Aldo Patocchi: "Per l'inaugurazione della mostra di Michele Cascella a *Villa Ciani*." *Realtá*, Naples, November 1954

Lionello Fiumi: "Michele Cascella." *Il Tirreno*, Leghorn, December 14, 1954

Erardo Aeschlimann: "Bibliografia del libro d'arte italiano." Carlo Bestetti Editore, Rome, 1954

David Burnard: "Leonor Fini et Michele Cascella." *La Nouvelle Revue de Lausanne*, Lausanne, November 17, 1954

André Kuenzi: "Michele Cascella et Leonor Fini." *La Gazette de Lausanne*, Lausanne, November 22, 1954

Fredi Chiappelli: "Exposition des peintres *Fini et Cascella*." Lausanne, November 15, 1954

Movie reel in color: *Tempo di pittura: Michele Cascella.* Directed by G. Guerrasio, Production Emilfilm, 1954

Lionello Fiumi: "Il regain di Michele Cascella." *Il Giornale*, Naples, January 22, 1955

G. C.: "Cascella." *La Nazione*, Florence, April 27, 1955

A. S.: "Cascella alla Galleria Spinetti di Firenze." *L'Unità*, Rome, April 30, 1955

Lionello Fiumi: "L'ora di Cascella." *Luisiada*, Oporto, April 1955

Henri Heraut: "Michel Cascella." *Journal de l'Amateur d'Art*, Paris, May 25, 1955

André Warnod: "Les arts... Cascella." *Le Figaro*, Paris, May 27, 1955

Romeo Penna: "I tre amori di Michele Cascella." *Settimo Giorno*, December 6, 1955

Orio Vergani: "Il piccolo Vasari: Michelone." *Corriere di Informazione*, Milan, December 8 and 9, 1955

Sutter Creek Bar, 1961. Collection Mr. and Mrs. Willis A. Roller, Los Altos Hills, California

24 x 36 ¼ inches

RAFFAELE CARRIERI: "Michele Cascella e gli itinerari parigini." *Epoca,* December 25, 1955

MICHELE CASCELLA: "Come divenni pittore." Excerpt from *Nuova Realtà,* Number 1, Review of the Rotary Clubs of Italy.

P. G.: "Michele Cascella da Giosi." *Rome,* Naples, January 17, 1956

CARLO BARBIERI: "Note d'arte." *Il Mattino,* January 20, 1956

ALFREDO SCHETTINI: "La mostra di Michele Cascella." *Corriere di Napoli,* January 20 and 21, 1956

H. H.: "Michel Cascella." *Journal de l'Amateur d'Art,* Paris, April 10, 1956

BONAVENTURA CALORO: "Un abruzzese a Parigi." *Tempo,* Milan, May 17, 1956

GHIL.: "L'arte in vetrina: Quasi mezzo secolo di pittura di Michele Cascella in una mostra ordinata alla Galleria Rotta." *Il Secolo XIX,* October 26, 1956

RENATO OLIVIERI: "È sempre domenica nei quadri di Cascella." *Grazia,* Milan, January 13, 1957

VINCENZO PAPI: "La tavolozza di Michele Cascella." *L'Avvenire del Mezzogiorno,* January 26 and 27, 1957

P. G.: "A la Galérie Malaval: Lumineuse Italie avec Michele Cascella." *La République de Lyons,* Lyons, May 15, 1957

—: "Le peintre Cascella à la Galérie Malaval." *L'Echo Liberté,* Lyons, May 21, 1957

The Golden Gate, San Francisco, 1960. Collection Ing. Angelo Farsura, Milan   30 x 39 ¼ inches

Orio Vergani: "A Portofino si progetta un 'convento' per i pittori." *Il Corriere della Sera*, Milan, August 14, 1957

Mario Bitonte: "Incontro con Michele Cascella, il pittore abruzzese di Portofino." *Corriere del Giorno*, September 21, 1957

Virgilio Guzzi: "Cascella alla 'Russo.'" *Il Tempo*, October 23, 1957

—: "Michele Cascella." *Il Giornale d'Italia*, October 26, 1957

Michele Biancale: "Michele Cascella alla Galleria 'Russo.'" *Momento Sera*, October 29, 1957

J. E.: "Fedele all'impressionismo l'abruzzese Michele Cascella." *Il Giornale del Mezzogiorno*, Rome, October 31, 1957

Leonardo Borgese: "Michele Cascella." *Corriere della Sera*, Milan, December 3, 1957

Lionello Fiumi: "Fantômes et vivants sur les côtes liguriennes." *Visages du Monde*, n. 96.

Carlo Delfino: "Cascella pittore del Tigullio." *Settimo Giorno*, Milan, December 14, 1957

The Gold Rush, 1961 39 ¼ x 59 inches

Giorgio Kaisserlian: "Il tempo di Cascella." *Rotosei*, Rome, October 22, 1957

Piero Scarpa: "Michele Cascella." *Il Messaggero*, Rome, October 24, 1957

—: "Michele Cascella." *XX Tribune des Nations*, Paris, April 25, 1958

Robert Vrinat: "Galérie André Weil." *Artaban*, April 11, 1958

Lionello Fiumi: "A Parigi il pittore di Portofino." *Il Corriere del Pomeriggio*, Genoa, April 28, 1958

André Warnod: "Michele Cascella." *Le Figaro*, Paris, May 5, 1958

Attilio Battistini: "Finezza di Cascella." *Cronache dell'Urbe*, Rome, November, 1958

Ubaldo Silvestri: "Tutto il Tigullio in una mostra di Michele Cascella." *Rotosei*, No. 48, November 28, 1958

—: *Autostrada del Sole: Acquarelli e disegni di Michele Cascella.* Edizioni d'Arte del Tigullio, Portofino, 1958 (out of print)

Georges Pillement: "Michele Cascella." *La Nef de Paris*, 1958

D. C.: "Michele Cascella." *Il Resto del Carlino*, Bologna, May 24, 1959

A. J. BLOOMFIELD: "At the Battlefront He Painted Flowers." *San Francisco News-Call Bulletin*, February, 1960

HOWARD BURKE: "Cascella Art Now Showing." *Los Angeles Examiner*, April 24, 1960

DAN SWINTON: "Here's the Signore Who Paints Air—Italy's Greatest Living Painter, Michele Cascella." *Los Angeles Mirror-News*, April 20, 1960

IRENE ALEXANDER: "New Gallery Show Introduces Italian Painter." *Monterey Peninsula Herald*, August 25, 1960

MONT.: "Michele Cascella Americano." *Corriere Lombardo*, November 29, 1960

GIORGIO KAISSERLIAN: "Michele Cascella." *Il Popolo*, December 3, 1960

L. R.: "Cascella alla Gussoni." *Avanti*, December 6, 1960

STEFANO GHIBERTI: "Piccola Galleria di 'Gioia,' Michele Cascella." *Gioia*, January 15, 1961

CAROLYN STRICKLER: "California Love Affair." *Los Angeles Examiner*, May 28, 1961

GIAMMARIO SGATTONI: "Michele Cascella." *Il Banditore Sud*, June, 1961

DAVID COWGER: "Italian Artist Cascella Transporting Palo Alto to Europe." *Palo Alto Times*, November 8, 1961

—: "Il pittore Michele Cascella è innamorato della California." *Italia*, San Francisco, November 16, 1961

ERCOLE CAROSELLI: "Arrivederci a Michele Cascella." *Italia*, San Francisco, December 9, 1961

MARIO PALLADINI: "Michele Cascella a New York." *Il progresso italo-americano*, New York, December 17, 1960

EMILY GENAUER: "Art Exhibition—M. Cascella." *New York Herald Tribune*, December 12, 1959

O'CONNOR: "Michael Cascella, Milan Artist in Bay Area." *The Monitor*, San Francisco, January 27, 1961

COSTANZO COSTANTINI: "Incontro romano con Michele Cascella - Un'America col sapore di casa scoperta da un pittore italiano." *Il Messaggero*, March 21, 1962

BRUNO MORINI: "Michele Cascella." *Giornale d'Italia*, March 30, 1962

PIERO SCARPA: "Michele Cascella." *Il Messaggero*, March 30, 1962

—: "Honored Guest." *Rome Daily American*, Rome, April 3, 1962

RAFFAELLO BIORDI: "Note d'arte da Roma, grandioso successo della Mostra di Michele Cascella." *Italia*, San Francisco, April 5, 1962

R. B.: "America vista por un artista europeo." *Histonium*, Buenos Aires, May 1962

SUE DONNAM: "An Italian Post-Impressionist Looks at the Gold Country." *San Francisco Sunday Chronicle*, June 10, 1962

EMANUELE CORREA D'OLIVERA: "Michele Cascella." *Accademia*, Rome, April 1962

JACK FRASER: "Top Italian Artist has Exhibit of Works at Foothill College." *San Jose Mercury News*, July 22, 1962

—: "Three 'Firsts' at Foothill Preview of Michele Cascella's Paintings." *Palo Alto Times*, July 16, 1962

PAMELA MARSH: "Michele Cascella." *Christian Science Monitor, The Home Forum*, September 25, 1962

American Ballerina, 1961. Collection Abe Ginsburg, Teaneck, New Jersey								30 x 39 ¼ inches

Small Market in Portofino, 1962. Collection Dr. Pietro Gambetta, Genoa 28 ¾ x 39 ¼ inches

The Yellow Car. Private Collection, Rome

Lorenzo Bocchi: "A Paris Exhibit by Michele Cascella." *Corriere della Sera*, Milan, October 4, 1964

Michele Cascella: *Quaderni della Galleria Santo Stefano.* Venice, September 1964

Bonaventura Caloro: "Michele Cascella da New York alla California." *Il Tempo*, Rome, October 10, 1964

Leonardo Borgese: "Michele Cascella." *Corriere della Sera*, November 24, 1964

Alberico Sala: "Cascella in una Mostra di Cinquant'Anni." *Amica, No. 49*, December 6, 1964

Martine Girbal: "Phantaisie Variété." Paris, December 1964

ONE-MAN SHOWS IN THE UNITED STATES SINCE 1959

New York City, N. Y., Chase Gallery, 1959
San Francisco, California, Maxwell Galleries, 1960
Beverly Hills, California, Acosta Galleries, 1960
Carmel, California, Laky Galleries, 1960
Stockton, California, Pioneer Museum and Haggin Galleries, 1960
Saratoga, California, Montalvo, 1961

Stanford, California, Stanford University Art Gallery, 1961
Fresno, California, Fresno Arts Center, 1961
Santa Clara, California, University of Santa Clara, de Saisset Art Gallery, 1961
San Francisco, California, W. & J. Sloane, Inc., 1961
Beverly Hills, California, Acosta Galleries, 1961
Boise, Idaho, The Boise Art Association, 1961
Seattle, Washington, Otto Seligman Galleries, 1961
Kansas City, Missouri, Group showing, William Rockhill Nelson Gallery of Art, Atkins Museum of Fine Arts, 1962
Sacramento, California, E. B. Crocker Art Gallery, 1962
Atherton, California, Decorators' Show, Villa Rosa, 1962
Foothill College, Los Altos, California, 1962
Woodside, California, Sharon Heights Country Club, 1963
Carmel, California, Laky Galleries, 1963
Beverly Hills, California, Acosta Galleries, 1963
Santa Clara, California, University of Santa Clara, de Saisset Art Gallery, 1963
Menlo Park, California, Atherton Gallery, 1963
San Antonio, Texas, William Glasser Gallery, 1964
Carmel, California, Laky Galleries, 1964
Woodside, California, Sharon Heights Country Club, 1964
Palo Alto, California, Crocker Citizens National Bank, 1964

Monastery of Michetti, Francavilla on-the-Sea

LIST OF
COLLECTORS OF CASCELLA ORIGINALS IN THE UNITED STATES

Mrs. Nelson Adams, *New York*

Mr. and Mrs. Pancho Alliati, *Las Vegas, Nevada*

Mrs. Hervé Alphand, *Washington, D.C.*

Mrs. Eleanor F. Anderson, *San Francisco, California*

Miss Gertrud Aronstein, *Palo Alto, California*

Mr. and Mrs. David T. Artson, *San Francisco, California*

Miss Mary E. Ashton, *El Cerrito, California*

Mrs. Lucille Athearn, *San Francisco, California*

Mr. and Mrs. W. R. Back, *Palo Alto, California*

Miss Louise T. Baer, *Stockton, California*

Mr. and Mrs. Joseph G. Balestra, *Atherton, California*

Mr. and Mrs. J. Merriam Barnes, *Detroit, Michigan*

Mr. and Mrs. Robert E. Berggren, *Sunnyvale, California*

Mr. and Mrs. Emilio Biordi, *San Francisco, California*

Mr. and Mrs. Allan Blumenfeld, *San Francisco, California*

Mr. and Mrs. Brown Bolté, *New Canaan, Conn.*

Mr. and Mrs. Marc L. Boss, *Palo Alto, California*

Mr. and Mrs. Nino Brambilla, *San Francisco, California*

Mr. and Mrs. Fred Brosio, *Los Angeles, California*

Mr. Dadid Bruce, *New York*

Mr. and Mrs. George Brunn, *Berkeley, California*

Mrs. Mary Connell Burroughs, *Santa Ana, California*

Mr. and Mrs. Paul F. Calabi, *Atherton, California*

Mr. and Mrs. Frank G. Chambers, *San Francisco, California*

Mr. and Mrs. Daniel Chapin, *Atherton, California*

Mrs. Helena Charlton, *Phoenix, Arizona*

Mr. and Mrs. Jack R. Clumeck, Jr., *San Francisco, California*

Mr. and Mrs. Samuel T. Cohen, *Hayward, California*

Mr. and Mrs. Louis P. Corbetta, *Los Altos Hills, California*

Dr. Ferruccio A. di Cori, *New York*

Mr. Oscar Cox, *Washington, D. C.*

Mrs. L. B. Crow, *Palo Alto, California*

Mr. and Mrs. I. W. Danielson, *Palo Alto, California*

de Saisset Art Gallery, University of Santa Clara, *Santa Clara, California*

Mr. and Mrs. Joe del Valle, *San Francisco, California*

Mr. Ralph L. Dickman, *Tacoma, Washington*

Mr. and Mrs. Lou Eaton, *Northridge, California*

Mr. François P. Elter, *New York*

Mr. and Mrs. Warren G. Epstein, *San Francisco, California*

Mr. and Mrs. Mortimer Fleishhacker, III, *San Francisco, California*

Mrs. Fletcher, *Los Angeles, California*

Miss Mary Elizabeth Forster, *Menlo Park, California*

Mrs. Sybil Forster, *Menlo Park, California*

French and Company, *New York*

Mr. Albert M. Gage, *San Francisco, California*

Mr. and Mrs. Ernest Gallo, *Modesto, California*

Mr. and Mrs. John R. Gardiner, Jr., *Kentfield, California*

Mr. and Mrs. H. M. Gardner, *Atherton, California*

Mr. and Mrs. K. A. Gardner, *Westport, Connecticut*

Mr. and Mrs. Abe Ginsburg, *Teaneck, New Jersey*

Mr. and Mrs. Joseph L. Gitterman, Jr., *New York*

Mr. William Glasser, *San Antonio, Texas*

Dr. and Mrs. Rubin L. Gold, *San Francisco, California*

Dr. and Mrs. Gilbert P. Gradinger, *San Mateo, California*

Dr. and Mrs. Cary P. Gray, *Portola Valley, California*

Mr. and Mrs. Z. Wayne Griffin, *Los Angeles, California*

Mr. William A. L. Guest, *San Francisco, California*

Dr. and Mrs. Morris Gutterman, *Palo Alto, California*

Mrs. Ruth Hansen, *Van Nuys, California*

Mr. Marco Heidner, *Tacoma, Washington*

Mr. and Mrs. Irving L. Heller, *Palo Alto, California*

Mr. and Mrs. Hoyt W. Herrald, *Atherton, California*

Mr. and Mrs. L. E. Hertzberg, *Chicago, Illinois*

Mr. and Mrs. Mortimer H. Herzstein, *San Francisco, California*

Dr. Stanley Hoffman, *Los Angeles, California*

Mr. and Mrs. Jay Holmes, *New York*

Dr. and Mrs. James H. Inglis, *Palo Alto, California*

Dr. and Mrs. John Ise, Jr., *Santa Barbara, California*

Mr. and Mrs. John J. Jacobs, *San Francisco, California*

Mr. and Mrs. Elmer A. Jensen, *Salinas, California*

Mr. and Mrs. H. Bradley Jones, *Pasadena, California*

Miss Marjorie F. Kahn, *Los Angeles, California*

Mr. and Mrs. Samuel Kalman, *San Francisco, California*

Mr. and Mrs. Max Kameny, *Oakland, California*

Mrs. Leon S. Kaplan, *New Britain, Connecticut*

Mr. and Mrs. John W. Keffer, *Coral Gables, Florida*

Dr. Hans H. Kohler, *Los Angeles, California*

Mrs. Isabel F. Lane, *Palo Alto, California*

Dr. and Mrs. Henry W. Lavendel, *Palo Alto, California*

Mr. and Mrs. Harlan Legro, *Los Gatos, California*

Mrs. Nita Lehane, *Palo Alto, California*

Mr. and Mrs. David K. Lightburn, *Palo Alto, California*

Mr. and Mrs. Boris Lochak, *New York*

Dr. and Mrs. James McConnell, *Portola Valley, California*

Mr. and Mrs. Neil McDaniel, *Oakland, California*

Mr. and Mrs. Anthony Maiullo, *Detroit, Michigan*

Countess Mara, *New York*

Mr. Gian-Carlo Menotti, *New York*

Mr. Lynn Millar, *Washington, D. C.*

Miss Patricia Miller, *New York*

Dr. T. A. Montgomery, *Berkeley, California*

Mr. and Mrs. Edwin H. Morse, *Palo Alto, California*

Mr. and Mrs. J. Philip Moses, *Bloomfield Hills, Michigan*

Mr. and Mrs. Joseph Anthony Maiullo, *Grosse Pointe, Michigan*

Mr. and Mrs. Cecil H. Murphree, *Castro Valley, California*

Mr. and Mrs. Arthur H. Nobbs, *San Mateo, California*

Mr. and Mrs. Dino Olivetti, *New York*

Mr. and Mrs. Martin Padway, *Beverly Hills, California*

Miss Joyce Passetti, *Menlo Park, California*

Mr. and Mrs. Wayne Pearson, *Santa Clara, California*

Mr. and Mrs. Albert L. Petri, *Palm Springs, California*

Mr. and Mrs. William A. Pomeroy, *San Francisco, California*

Miss Jean Puffer, *Oakland, California*

Mr. Ronald Reagan, *Los Angeles, California*

Mrs. Eugene Rickansrud, *Los Altos, California*

Miss Ruth Rickansrud, *Berkeley, California*

Mrs. Frances Rilla, *Kentfield, California*

Mrs. Margot Robson, *Atherton, California*

Mr. Allard Roen, *Las Vegas, Nevada*

Mr. and Mrs. Willis A. Roller, *Los Altos Hills, California*

Mr. and Mrs. Robert Rose, *Piedmont, California*
Mr. Bernie Rothkopf, *Las Vegas, Nevada*
Mrs. Marcus Rothschild, *New York*
Dr. and Mrs. Frank C. Ruys, *Woodside, California*
Mr. and Mrs. Kurt Salmon, *Washington, D. C.*
Mr. Elmer Sammonds, *New York*
Mrs. Vern Schath, *Palo Alto, California*
Mr. and Mrs. Gilbert Schnitzer, *Portland, Oregon*
Mr. and Mrs. James J. Scoppettone, Jr., *Campbell, California*
Mr. and Mrs. Robert Seligson, *Oakland, California*
Mr. and Mrs. Sidney C. Seligson, *Los Angeles, California*
Mr. and Mrs. Angelo Servi, *Palo Alto, California*
Mrs. Mary Lee Shephard, *Atherton, California*
Mr. and Mrs. Walter H. Shorenstein, *San Francisco, California*
Mr. and Mrs. Julian Silverstein, *Teaneck, New Jersey*
Mr. and Mrs. John R. Simpson, Jr., *Longmeadow, Massachusetts*
Mr. and Mrs. George Solari, *San Francisco, California*
Mr. A. M. Sonnabend, *Boston, Massachusetts*
Mr. and Mrs. Leonard R. Spalding, *Portola Valley, California*
Mr. and Mrs. Harold Spitz, *San Francisco, California*
Mr. Cornelius V. Starr, *New York*
Mr. Alan Stearns, *Fort Lauderdale, Florida*
Mrs. Irene Steel, *Menlo Park, California*
Mr. George A. Strong, *Santa Clara, California*
Dr. and Mrs. Ernest Sultan, *Woodside, California*
Mr. and Mrs. Zyg Taube, *Los Angeles, California*
Mr. and Mrs. W. F. Taylor, *Los Angeles, California*
Mr. and Mrs. William A. Ternes, *Grosse Pointe, Michigan*
Mr. and Mrs. Stuart L. Treon, *Sunnyvale, California*
Mr. and Mrs. Leonard Unger, *San Francisco, California*
Mr. and Mrs. Stephen W. Veitch, *Atherton, California*
Mrs. Michael W. Vincent, *Berkeley, California*
Mrs. Doheny Washington, *Los Angeles, California*
Mrs. Gerda M. Weiden, *Atherton, California*
Mr. and Mrs. Lawrence D. West, *Palo Alto, California*
Mr. and Mrs. A. J. White, *Beverly Hills, California*
Mr. and Mrs. Walton A. Wickett, *Atherton, California*
Mr. and Mrs. Nathan Wolfson, *Beverly Hills, California*
Miss Jane Wyman, *Beverly Hills, California*
Mr. and Mrs. John J. v. W. Zaugg, *San Mateo, California*
Mr. and Mrs. Fred Zinnemann, *Los Angeles, California*

Mrs. Sybil Forster, Menlo Park, California   22 x 28 inches

Little Francesca, Palo Alto, California.   Collection Mrs. Sybil Forster, Menlo Park, California   22 x 28 inches

The Poet Clemente Rebora. Collection Society of Friends of Clemente Rebora   16 x 20 inches

The Cathedral at Guardiagrele (Abruzzo), 1965   32 x 40 inches

Piazza San Marco, Venice (watercolor), 1964. Private Collection, Beverly Hills, California   20 x 26 inches

The Home of Wally Toscanini, Venice (watercolor), 1964   20 x 26 inches

The Harbor of Ortona (Abruzzo), 1965   29 x 46 inches

Pont des Arts, Paris (watercolor), 1964. Collection Dr. Carlo Giudici, Milan   20 x 26 inches

The Convent at Guardiagrele (Abruzzo), 1965　　　　　　　　　　　　　　　　29 x 40 inches

New York, Fifth Avenue (at 60th), 1959 - oil.   Collection Mrs. Marcus Rothschild, New York   30 x 40 inches

56

PLATES

PLATE I: *White Dwellings* (pastel), 1909   19 ¾ x 23 ½ inches

M. Cascella 1915

PLATE II: *Russian Soldiers*, 1915

19 ¾ x 23 ½ inches

PLATE III: *The Artist's Mother*, 1923   25 ¼ x 29 ¼ inches

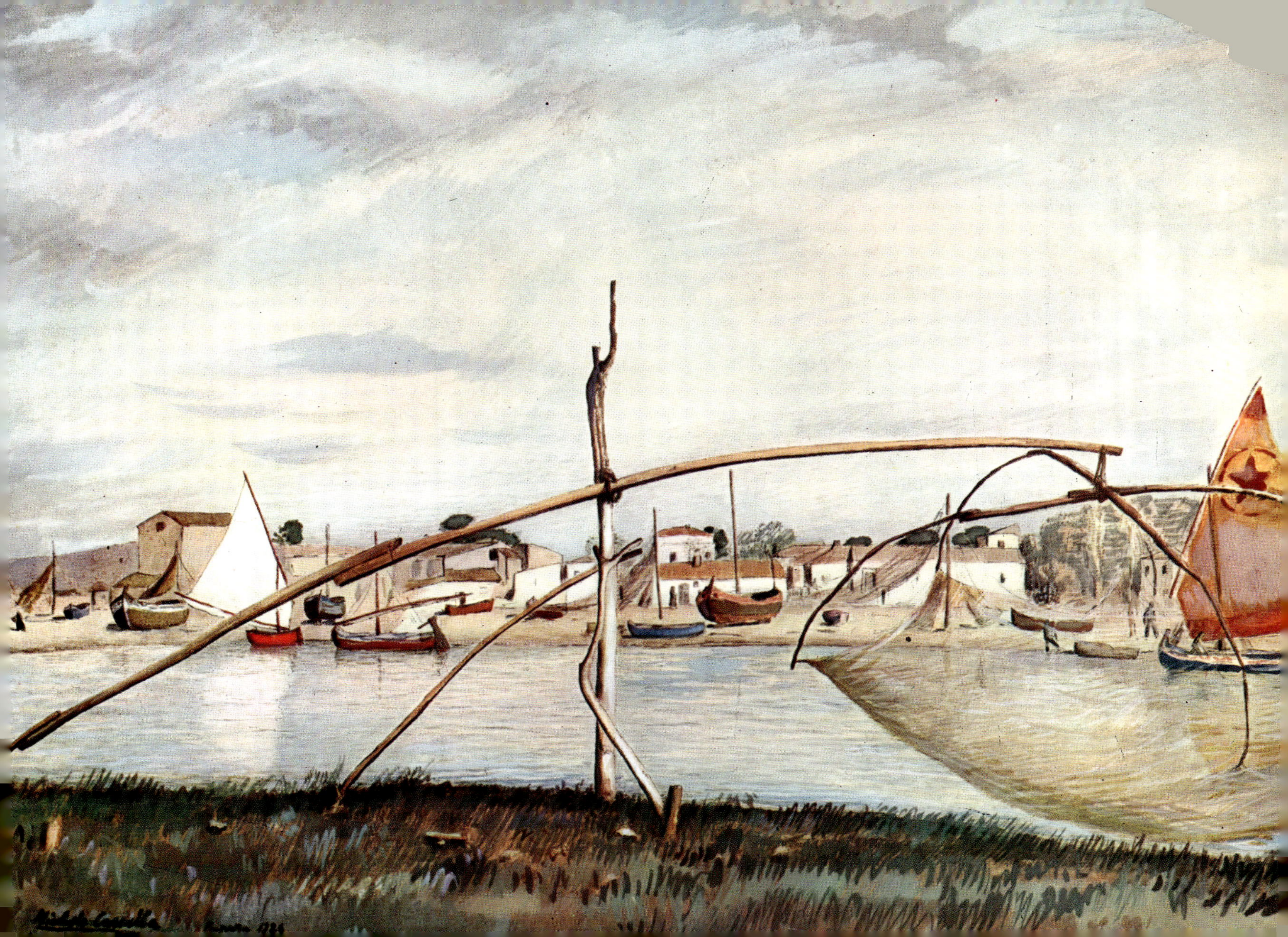

PLATE IV: *The River Pescara*, 1923   20 ⅞ x 29 ½ inches

PLATE V: *Canonization of Andrea Uberto Fournet*, 1933   55 x 59 inches

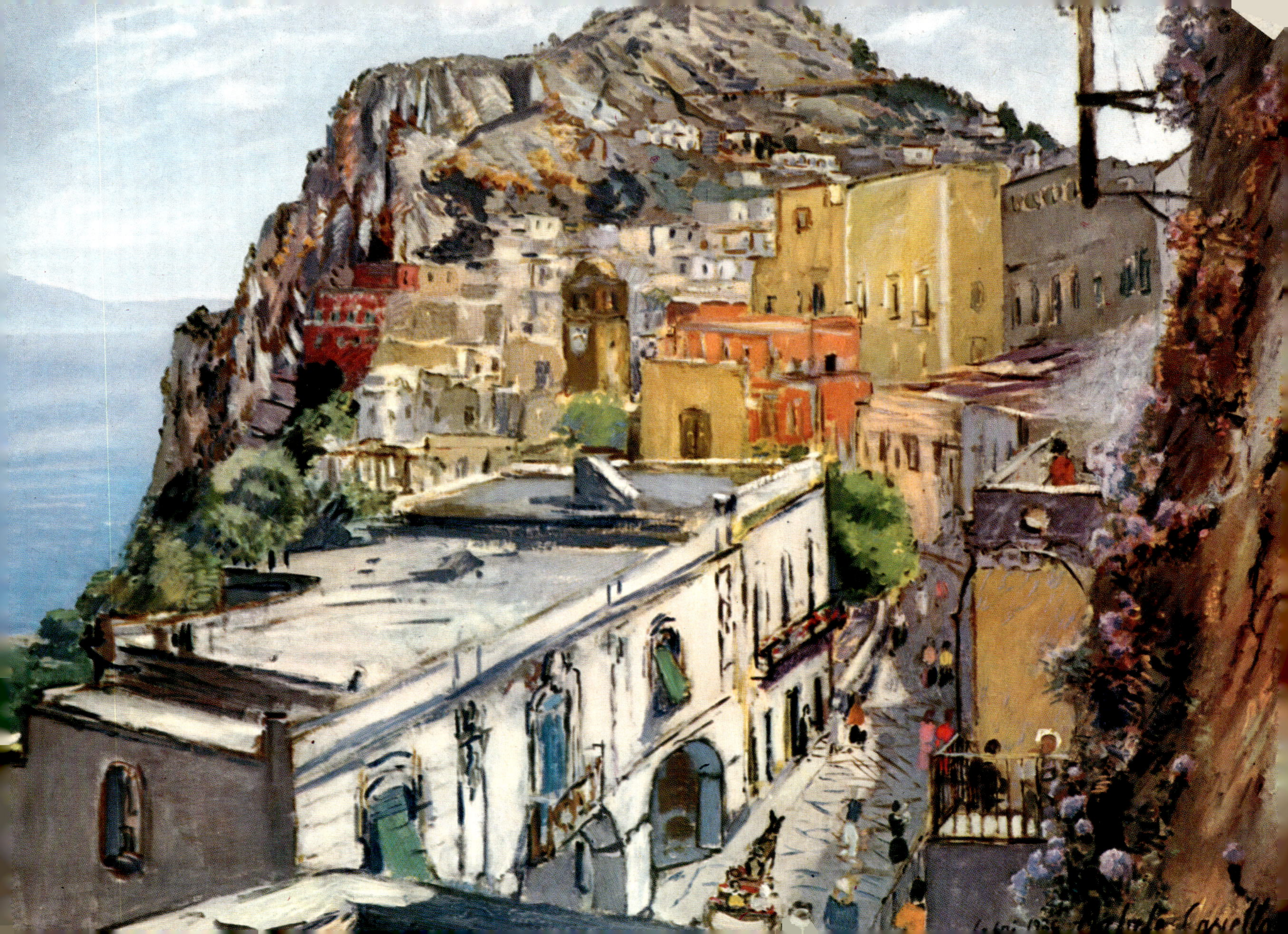

PLATE VI: *Capri,* 1935   37 x 51 inches

PLATE VII: *Flowers for Martha.* Collection André Toriel, Lausanne   28 ¾ x 39 ⅜ inches

PLATE VIII: *Window at Portofino*, 1957. Collection Julian Silverstein, North Bergen, New Jersey
35 x 57 ½ inches

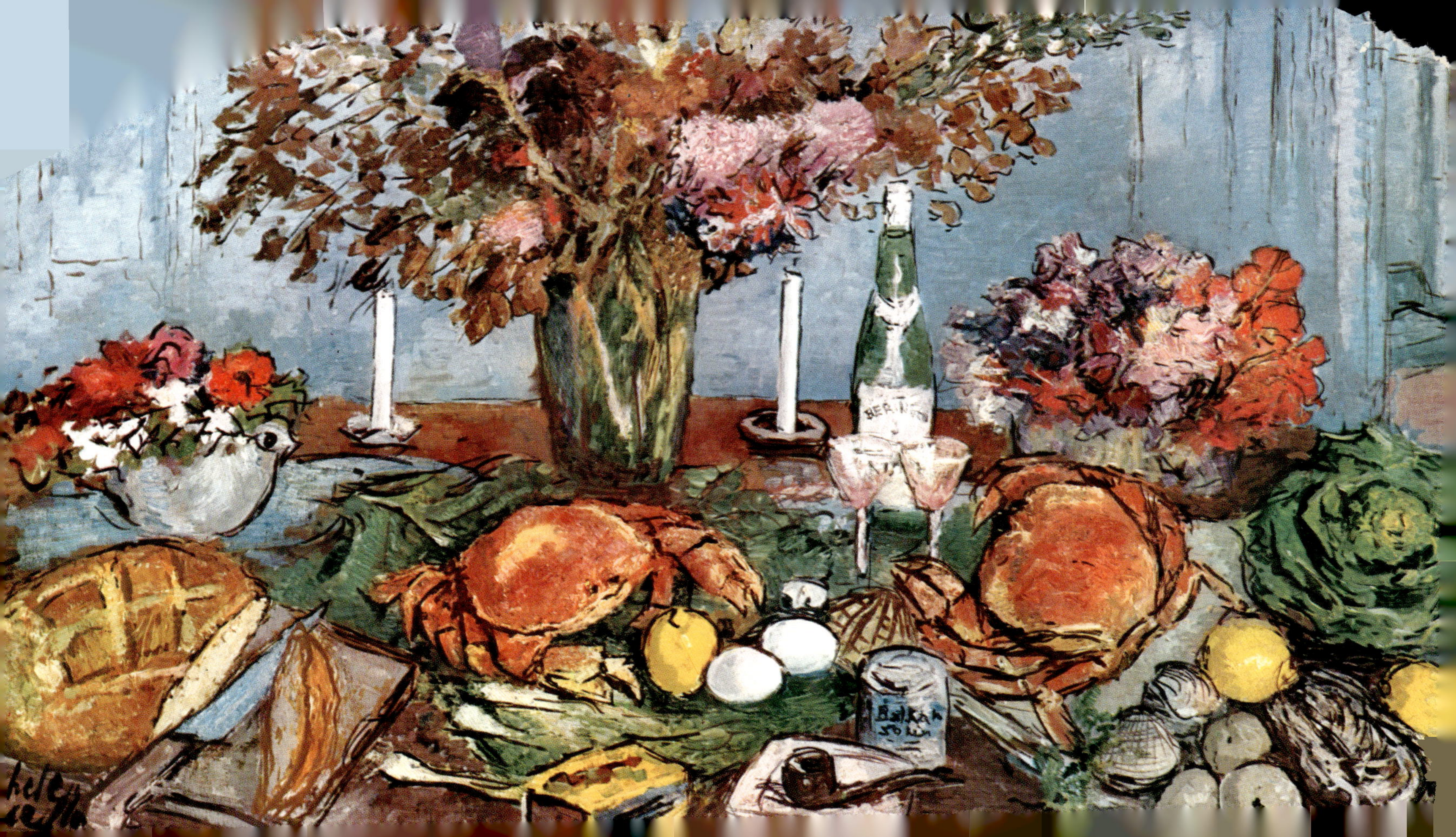

PLATE IX: *Dinner Table in California,* 1960 33 x 60 inches

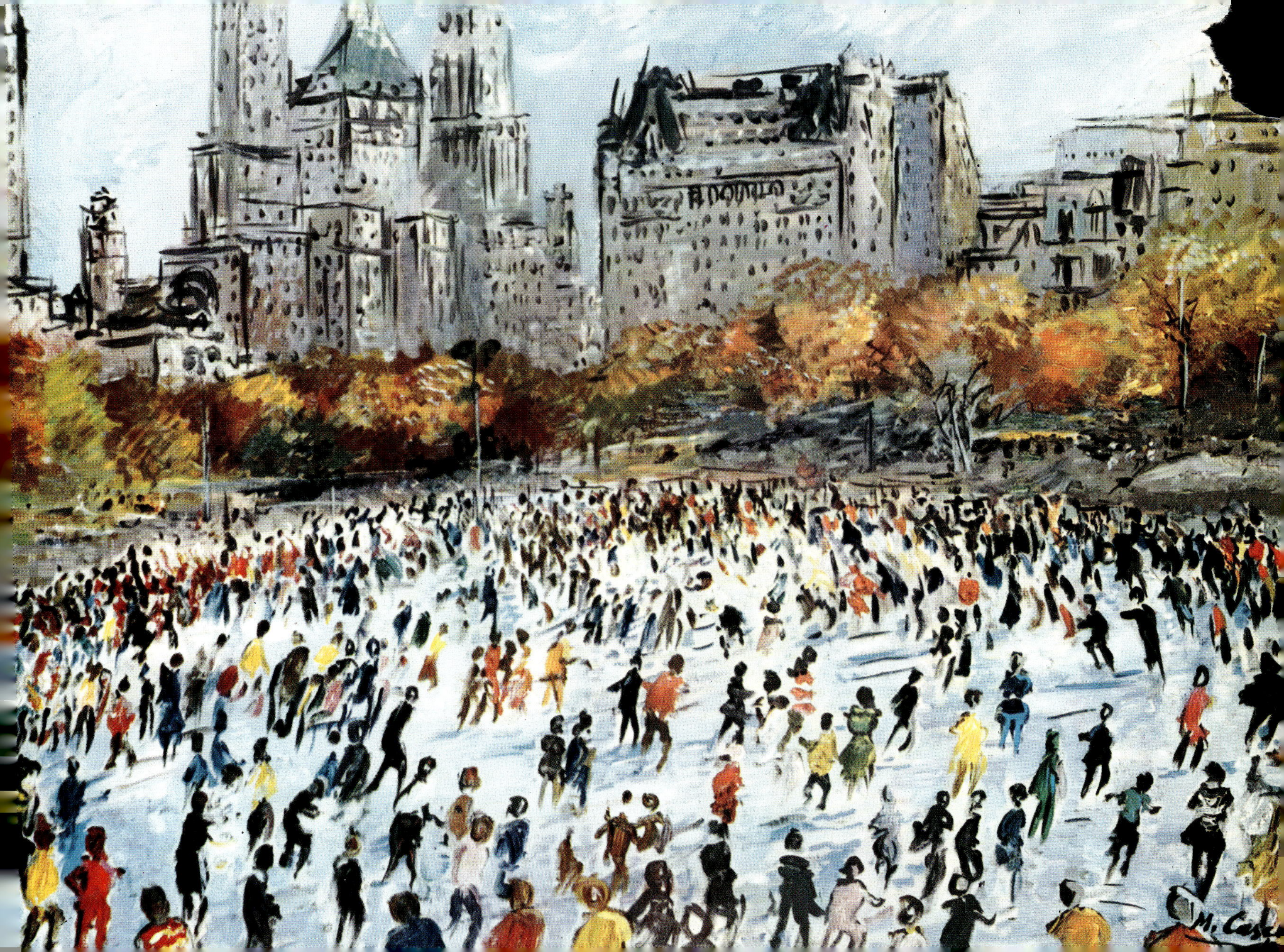

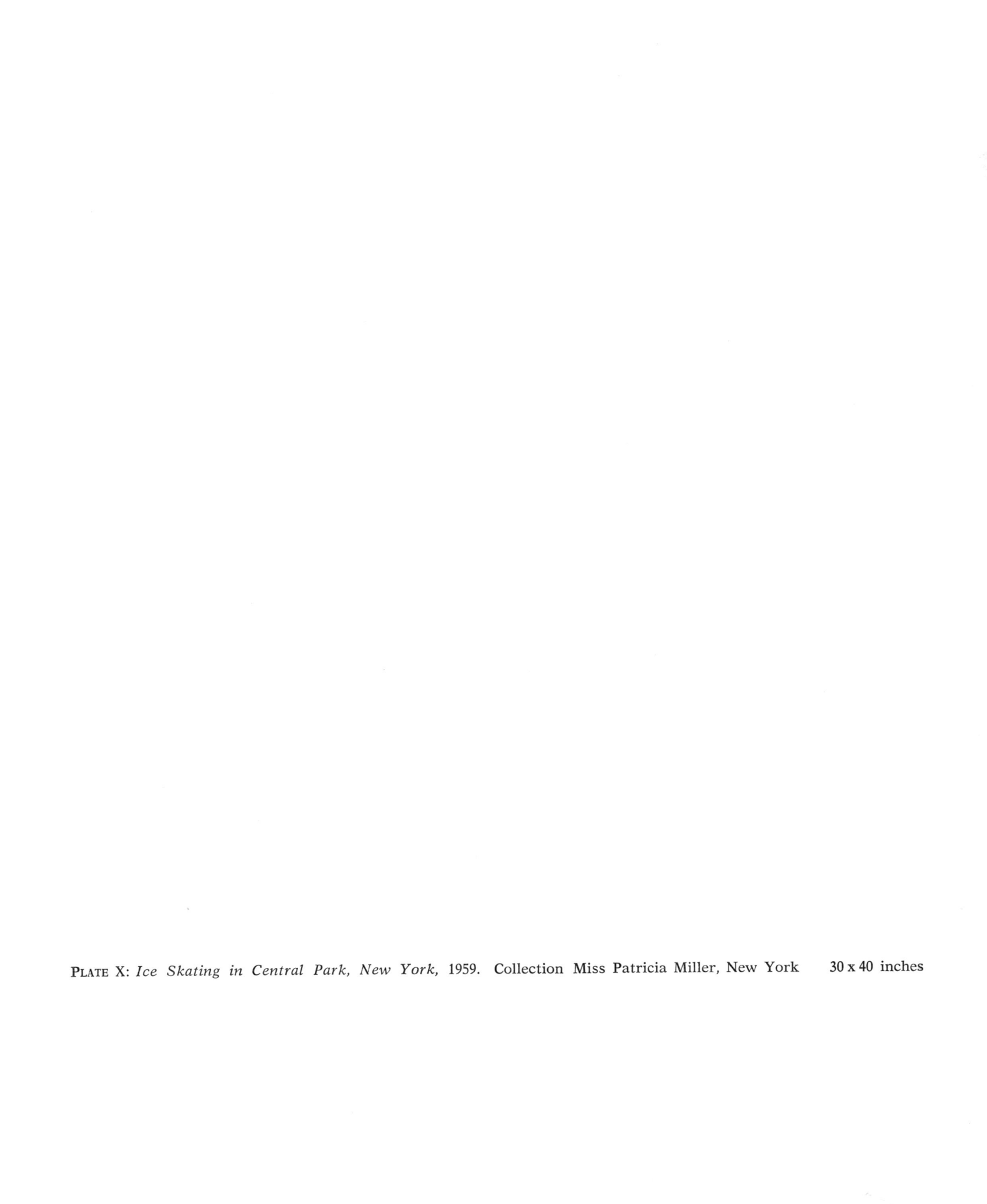

PLATE X: *Ice Skating in Central Park, New York*, 1959. Collection Miss Patricia Miller, New York   30 x 40 inches

PLATE XI: *Path of Lilies*, 1949. Collection Dr. Pietro Gambetta, Genoa

29 ½ x 43 ¼ inches

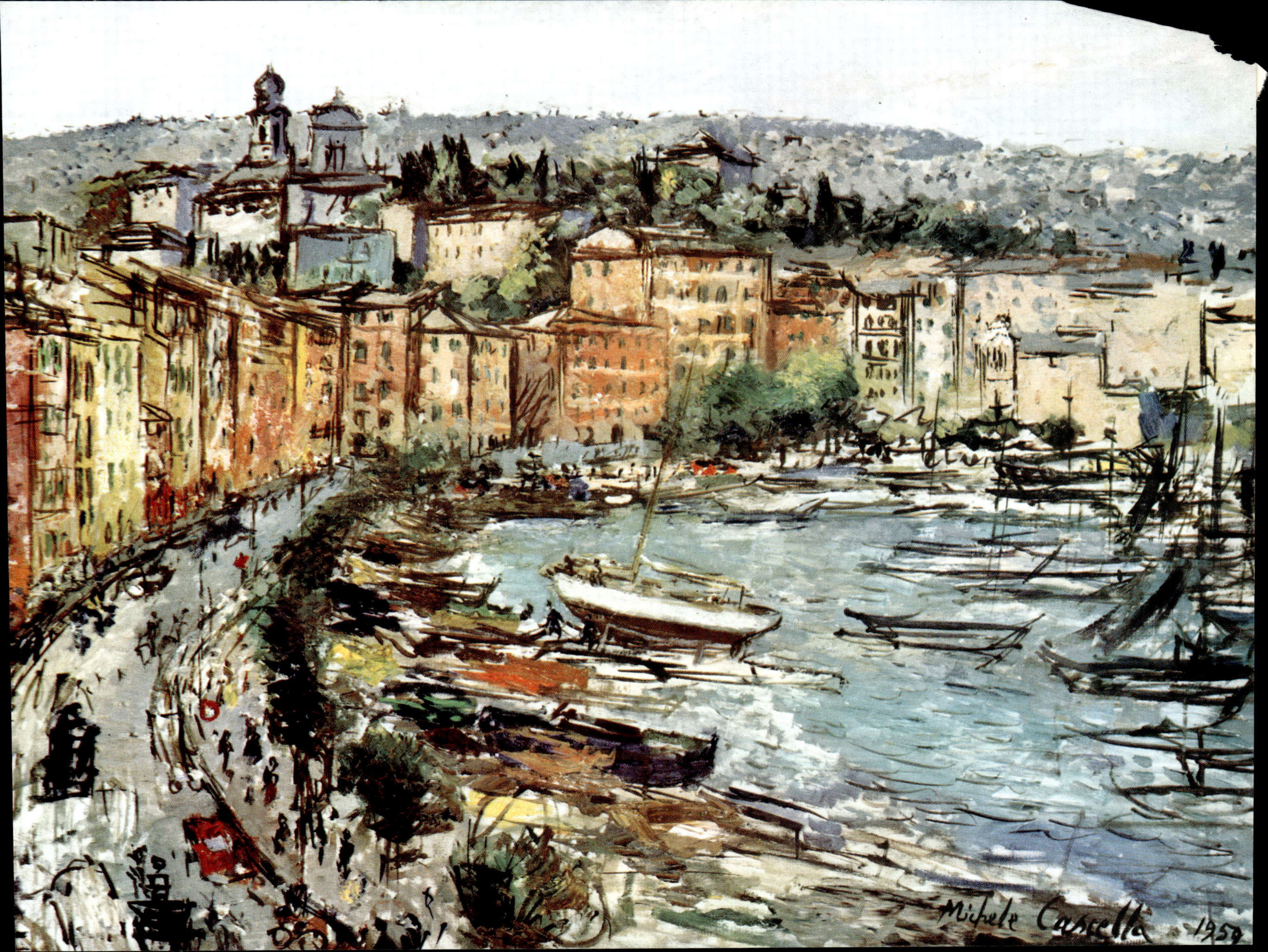
Michele Cascella 1959

PLATE XII: *Santa Margherita Ligure*, 1959. Collection William Glasser, San Antonio, Texas   30 x 39 ⅝ inches

Michele Cascella, Portofino 1960

PLATE XIII: *The Arcades in Portofino*, 1960. Collection Mrs. Helena Charlton, Phoenix, Arizona   28 ¾ x 39 ⅜ inches

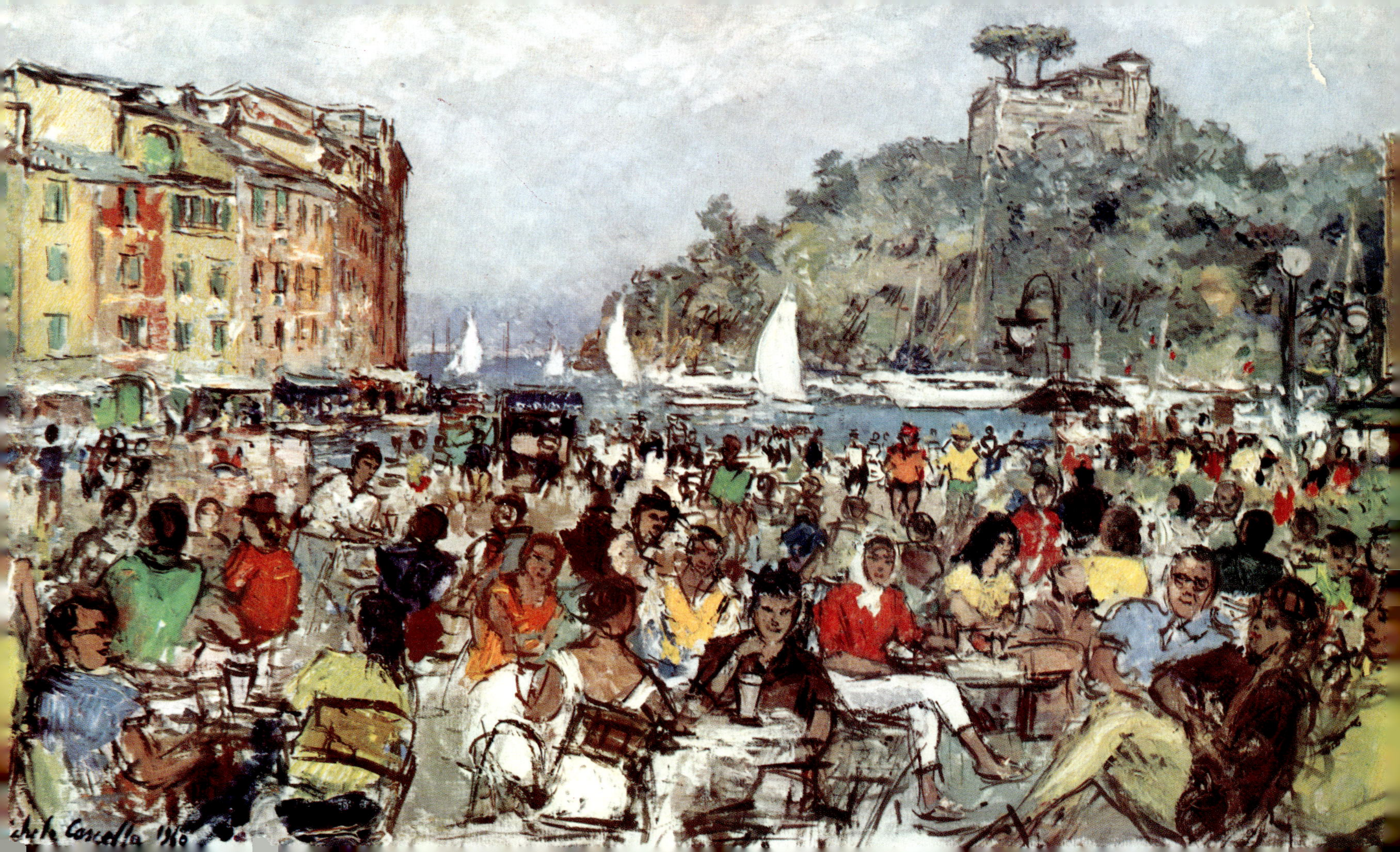
Cascella 1960

PLATE XIV: *People at Portofino,* 1960. Collection Ing. Lino del Favero, Milan 30 x 50 inches

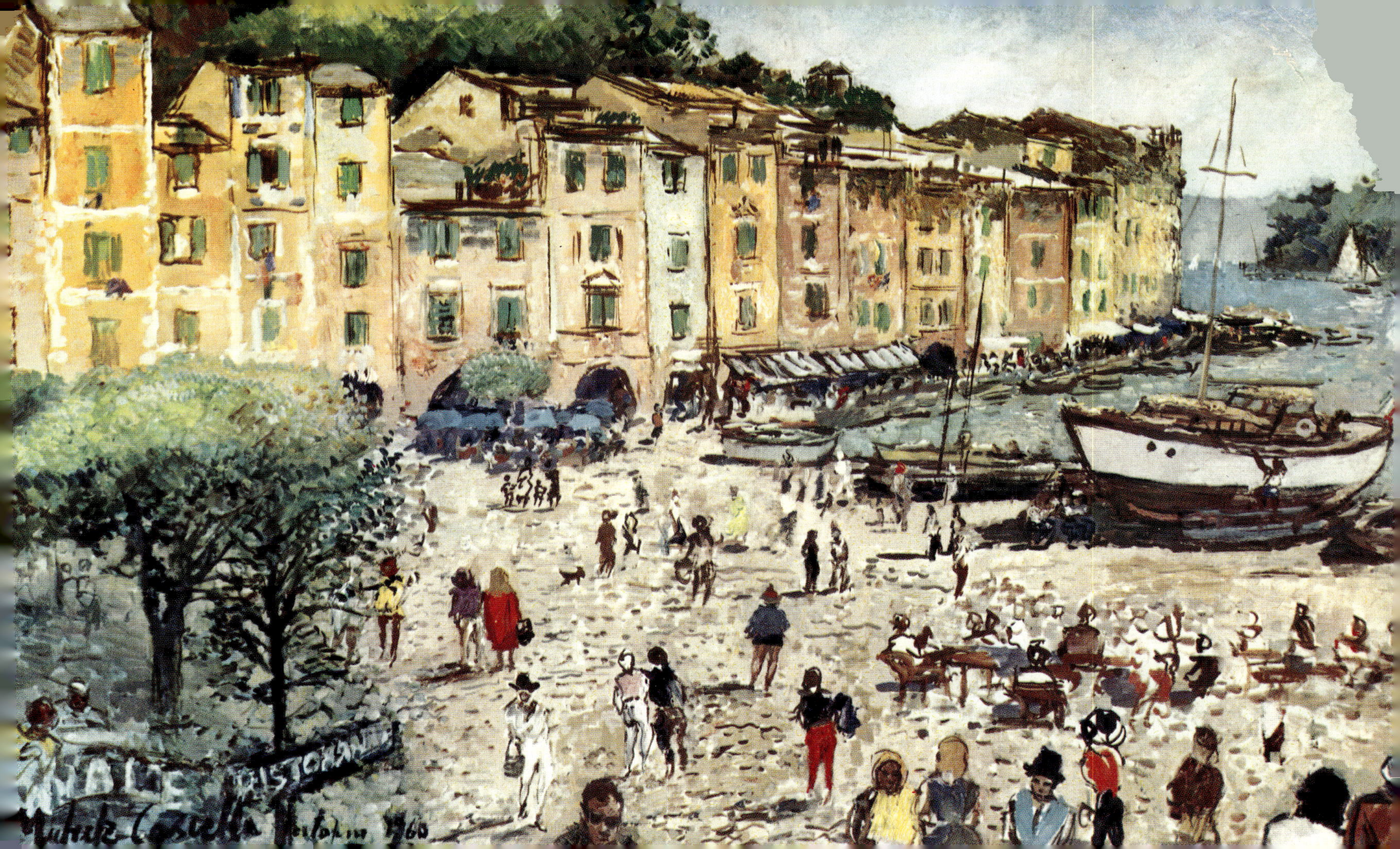
1960

PLATE XV: *Piazza in Portofino,* 1960. Collection Ralph L. Dickman, Tacoma, Washington   30 x 50 inches

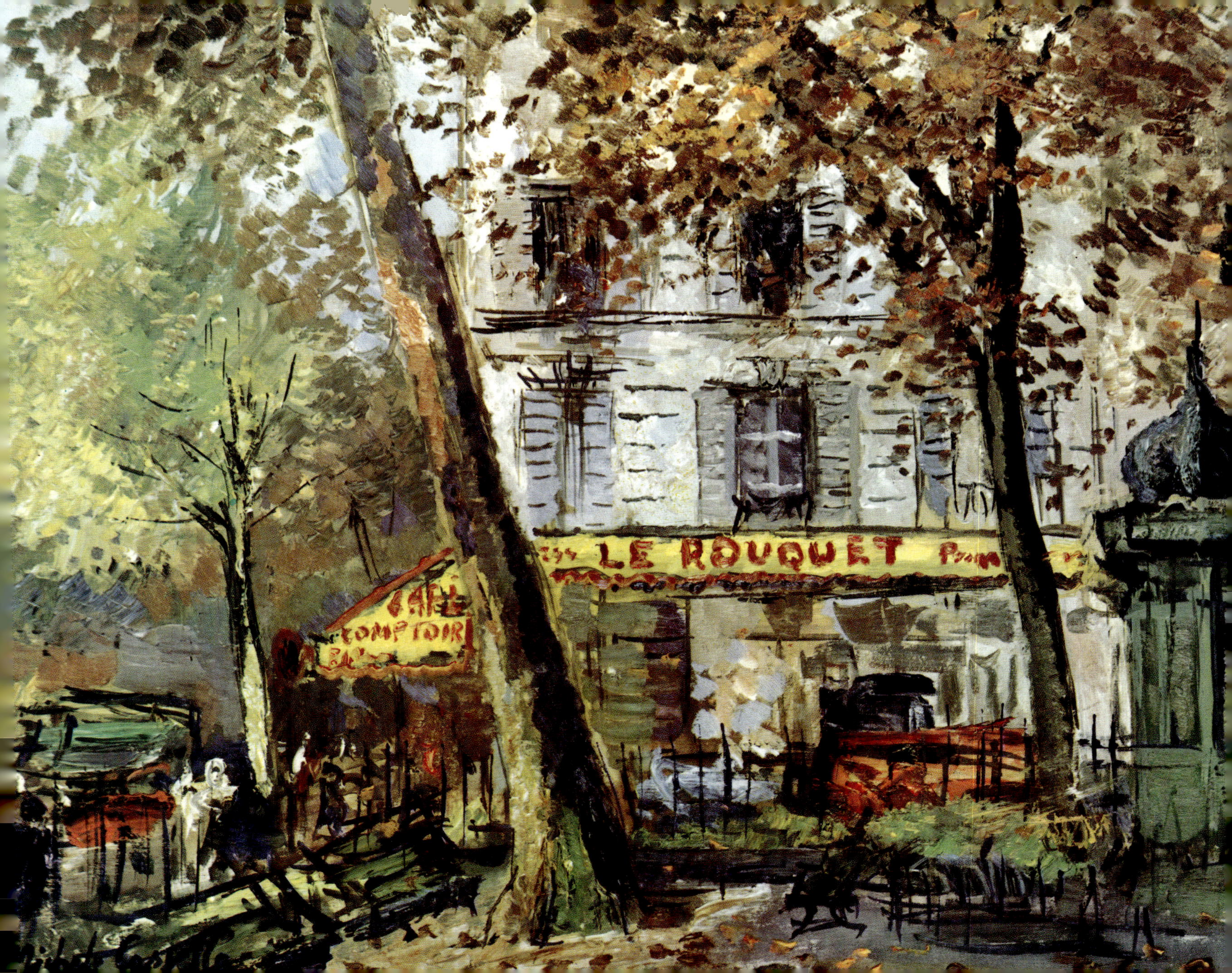
LE ROUQUET
COMPTOIR

PLATE XVI: *Café Le Rouquet, Paris,* 1960. Private Collection, Venice   22 x 28 inches

PLATE XVII: *Obsession of New York*, 1961   39 ⅜ x 59 ¼ inches

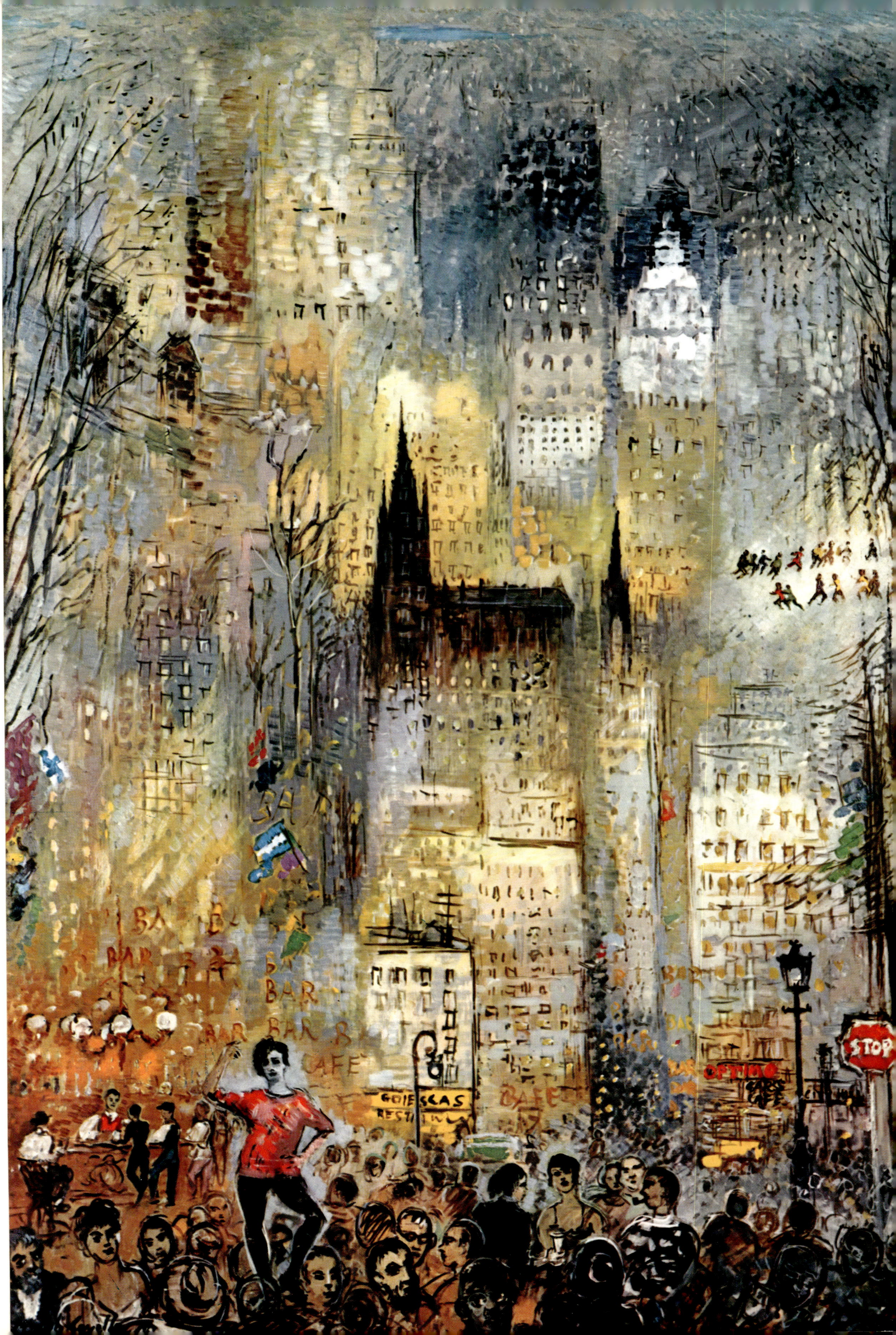

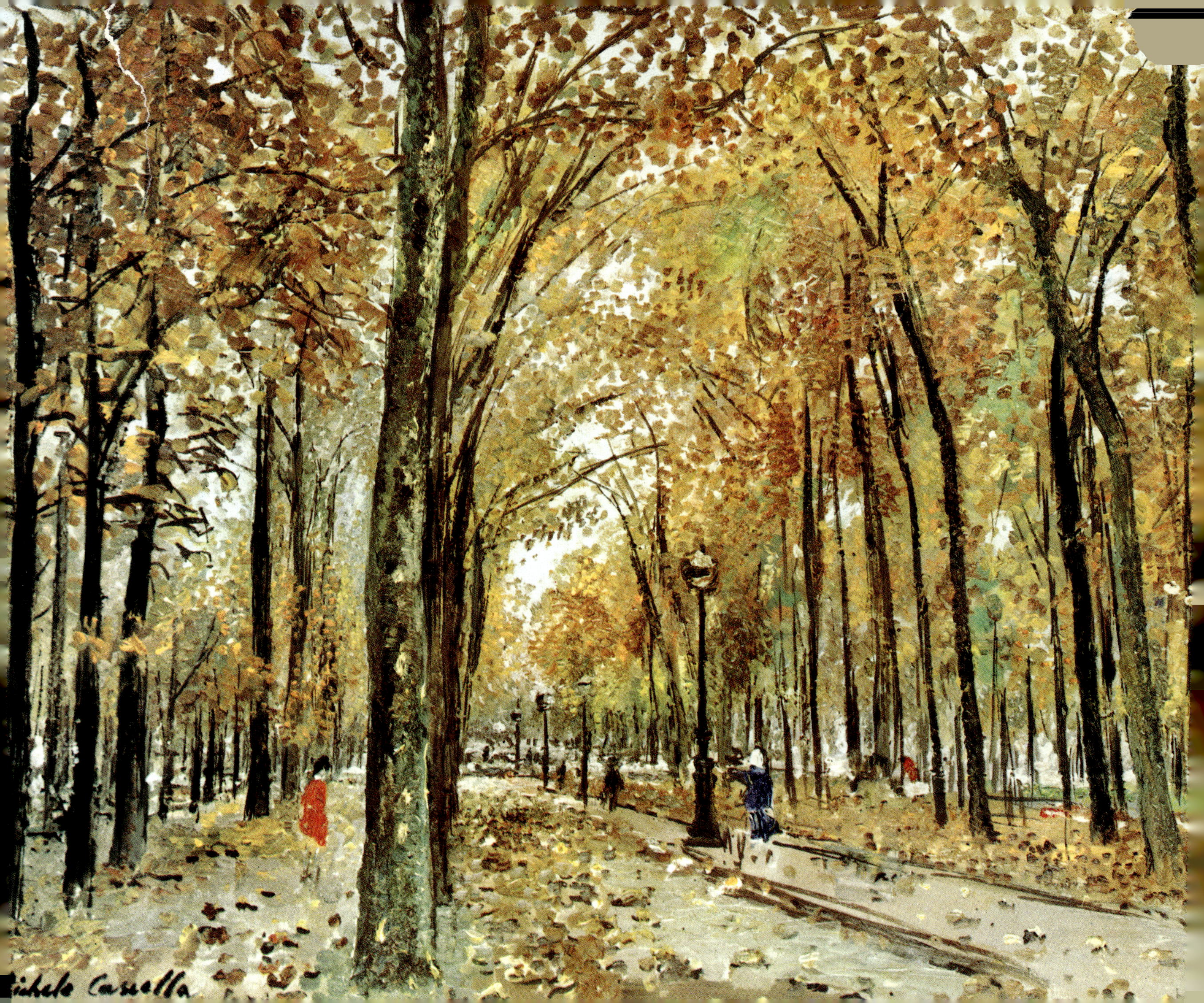
Cascella

PLATE XVIII: *Tuileries, Paris*, 1960. Collection Dr. and Mrs. Max Kameny, Oakland, California   30 x 39 ⅜ inches

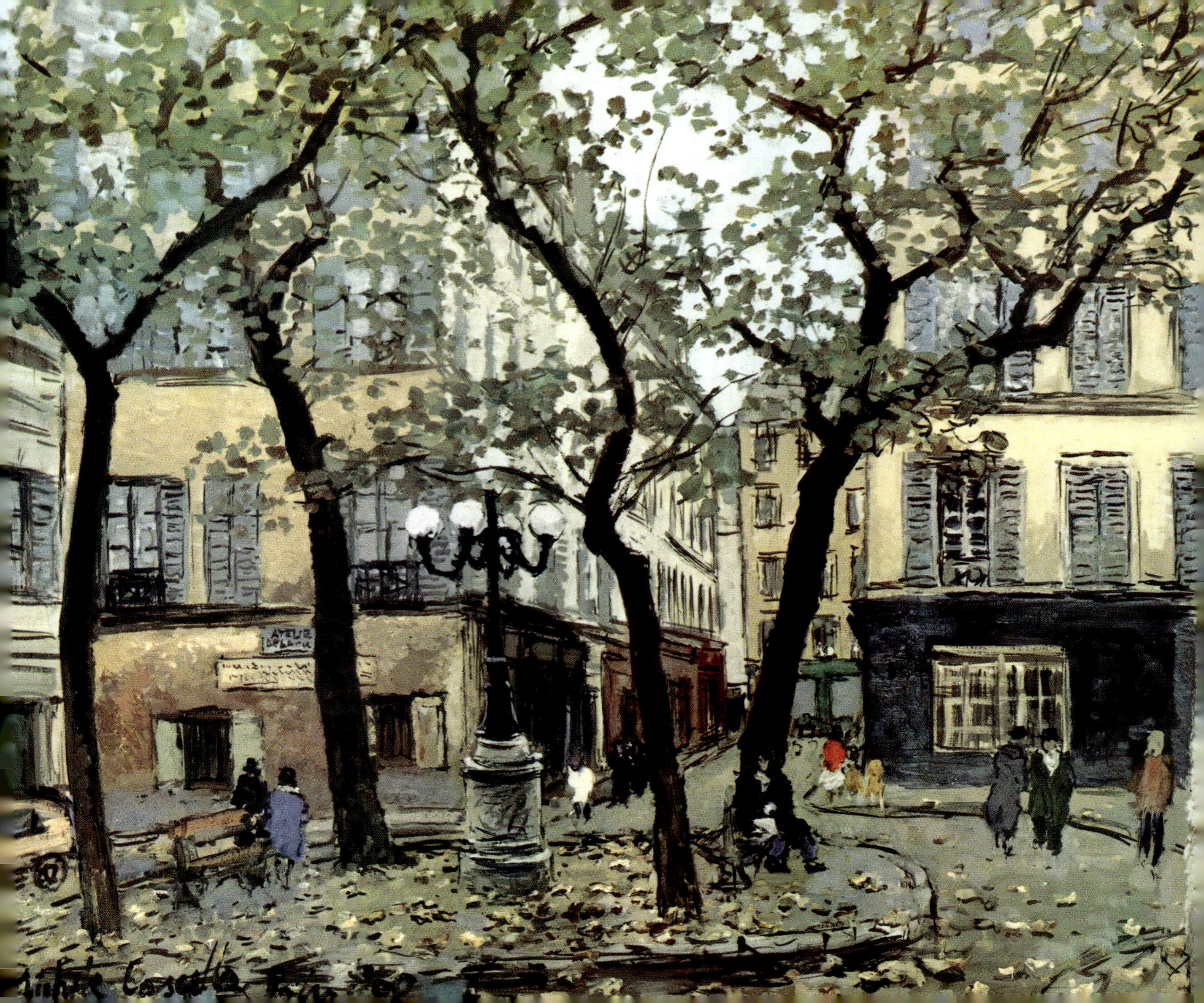

PLATE XIX: *Place Furstenberg, Paris,* 1960.   Collection Marco Heidner, Tacoma, Washington   30 x 39 ⅝ inches

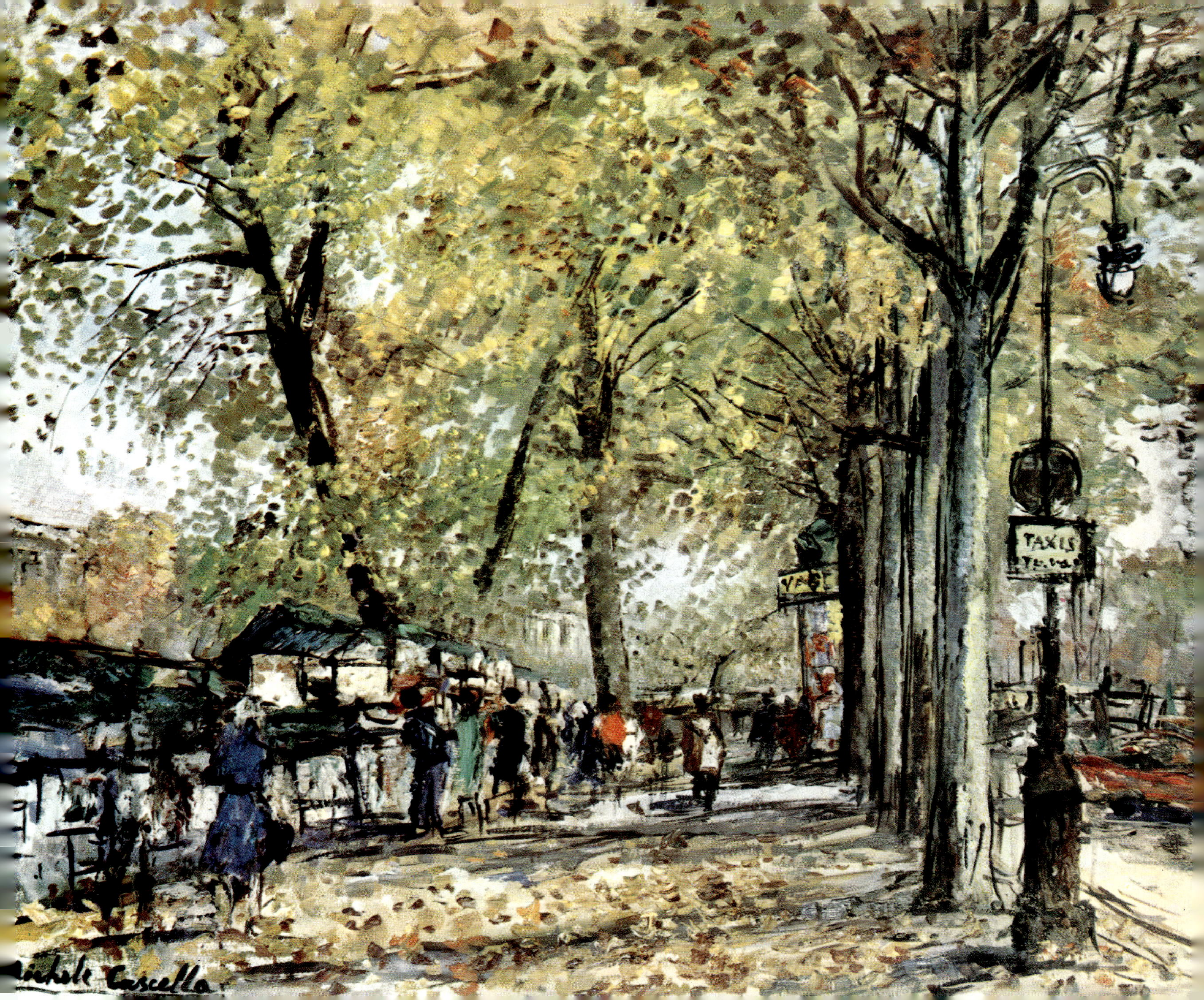
TAXIS
Cascella

PLATE XX: *Parisian Autumn*, 1959. Collection Mr. & Mrs. H. Bradley Jones, Pasadena, California   30 x 39 ⅝ inches

PLATE XXI: *Piazza d'Arquata Scrivia*, 1959. Collection Ing. Walter Comani, Pescara   28 ¾ x 45 ¼ inches

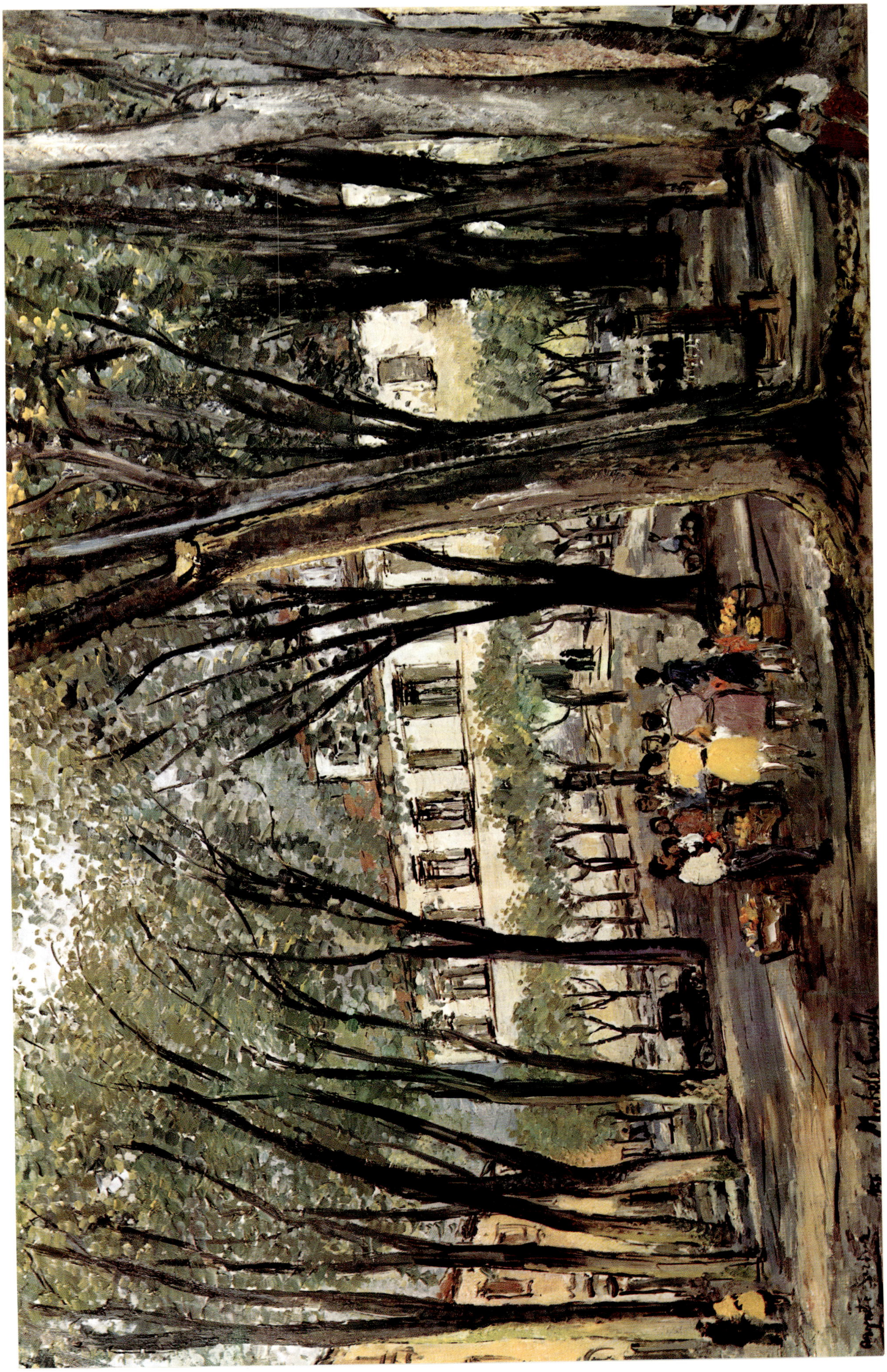

N.Y. 1958 Michele Cascella

PLATE XXII: *New York Public Library*, 1959. Collection Sergio Bonelli, Milan 30 x 39 ⅝ inches

PLATE XXIII: *Flowers of California*, 1961. Collection Mrs. Luisa Peretti, Rome   30 x 39 ⅜ inches

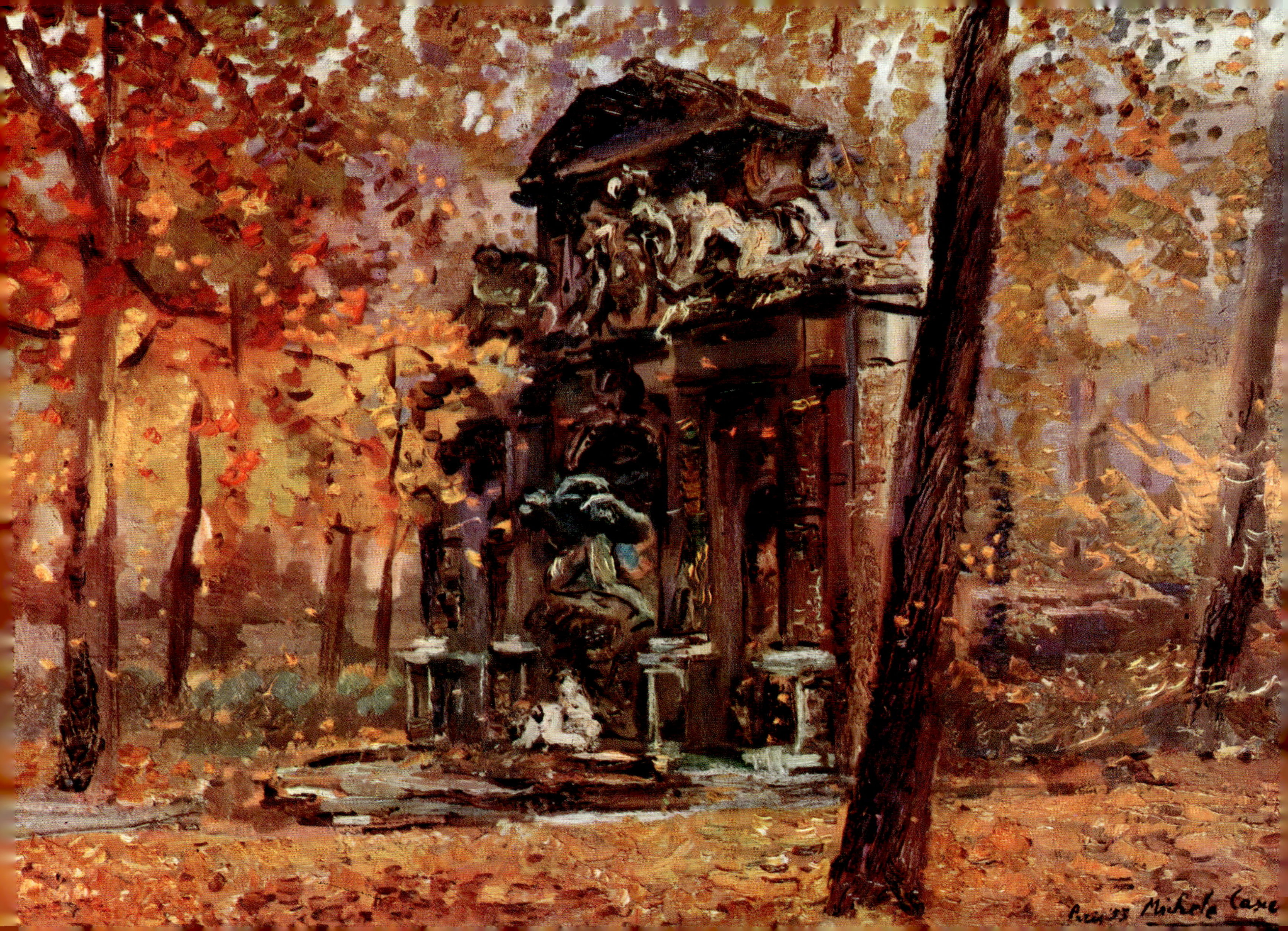

PLATE XXIV: *The Medici Fountain, Luxembourg Gardens, Paris.* Collection Mrs. Matilde Monzino, Milan 19 ⅝ x 27 ½ inches

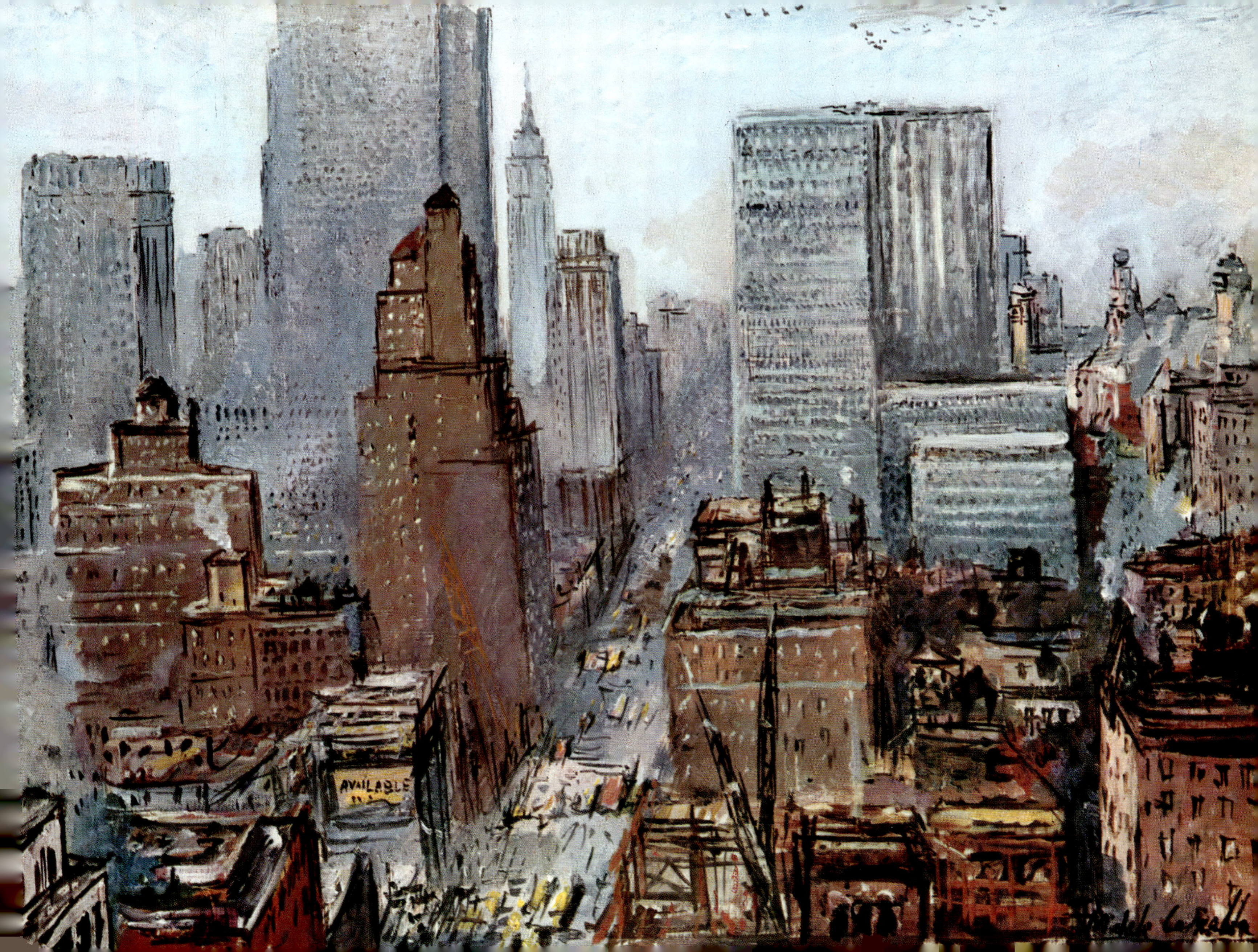
AVAILABLE

PLATE XXV: *Sixth Avenue, New York,* 1962   28 ¾ x 39 ⅜ inches

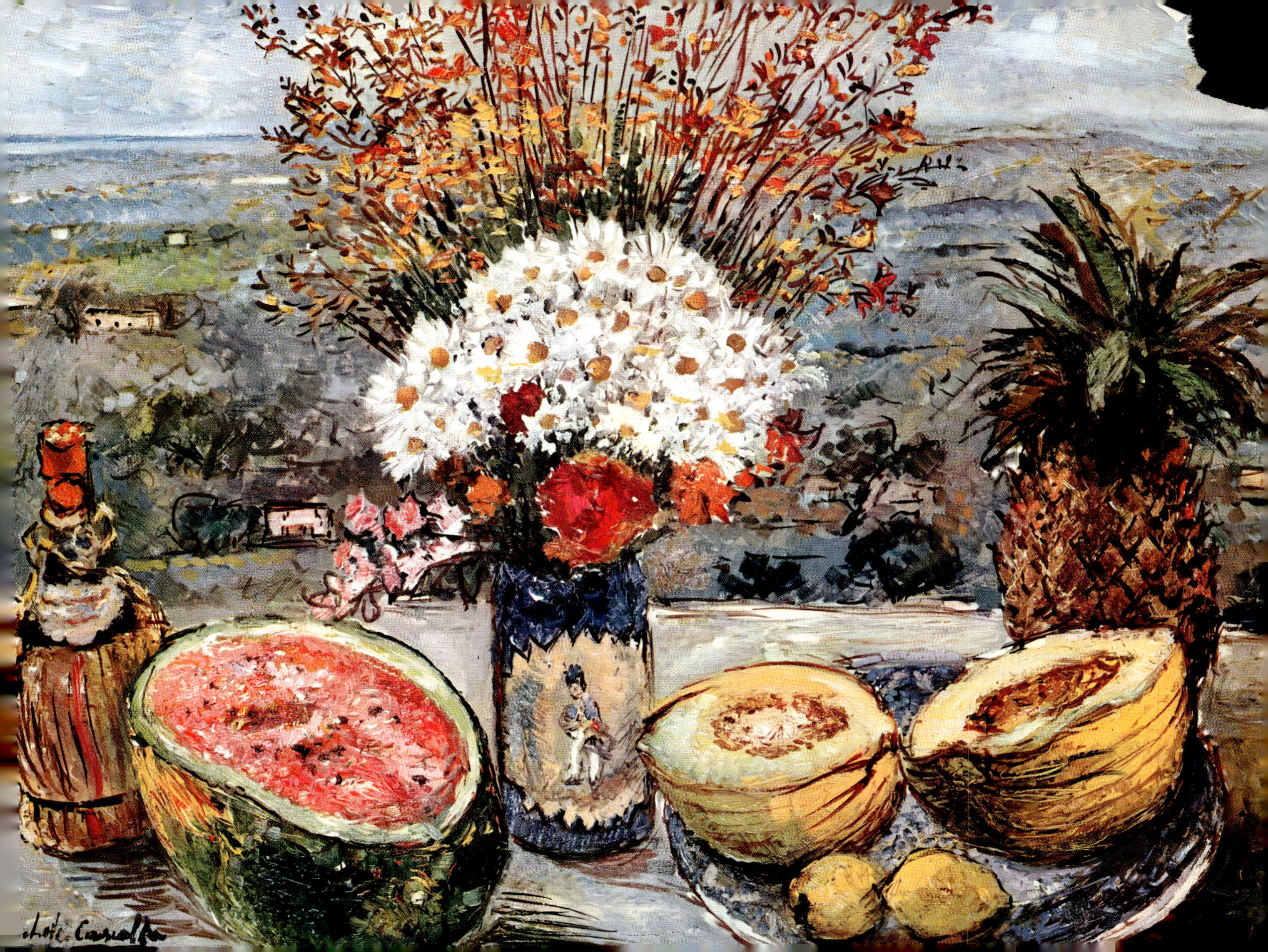

PLATE XXVI: *The Promised Land,* 1961. Private Collection, Hamburg   30 x 39 ⅜ inches

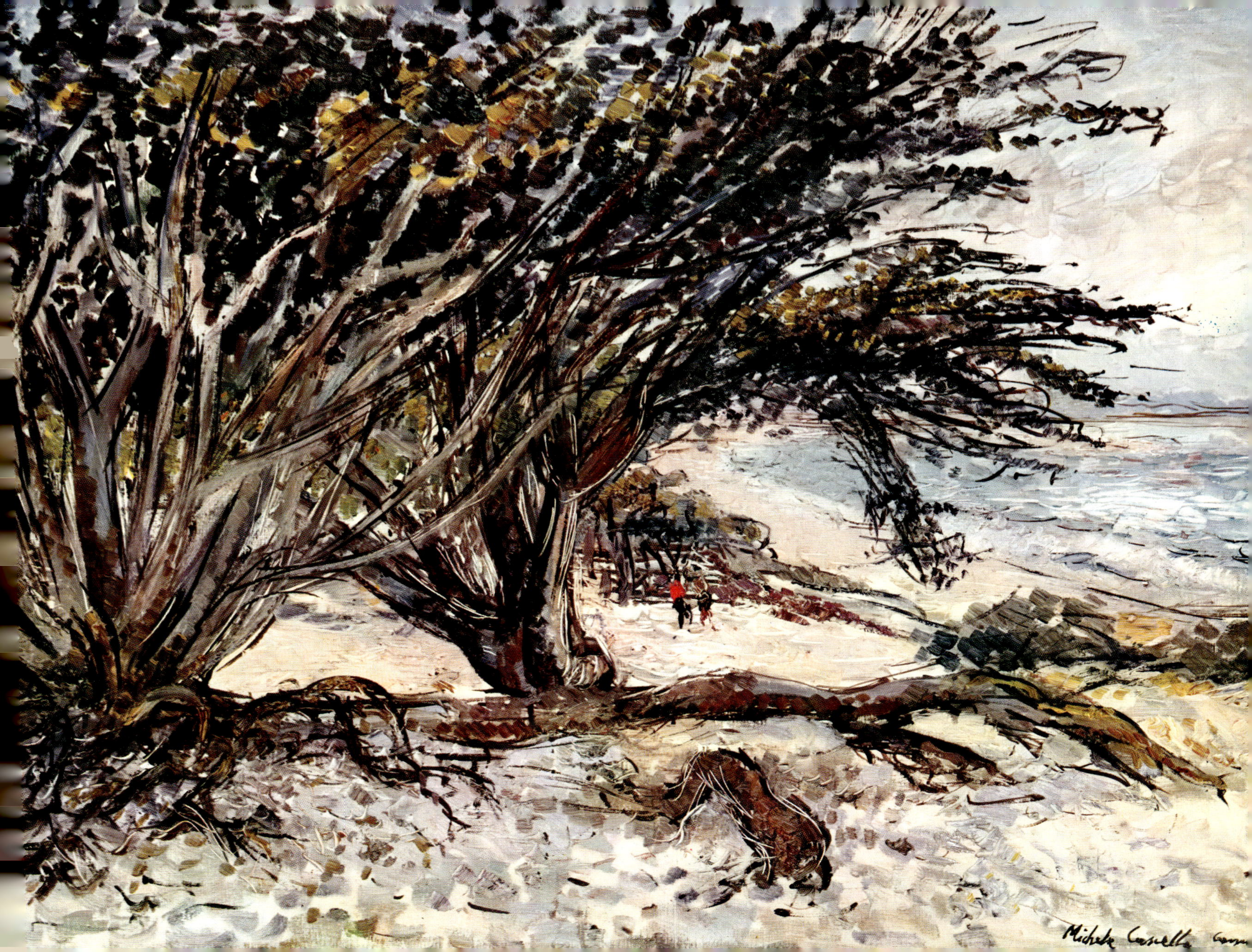

PLATE XXVII: *The Carmel Beach, California,* 1961   30 x 39 ⅝ inches

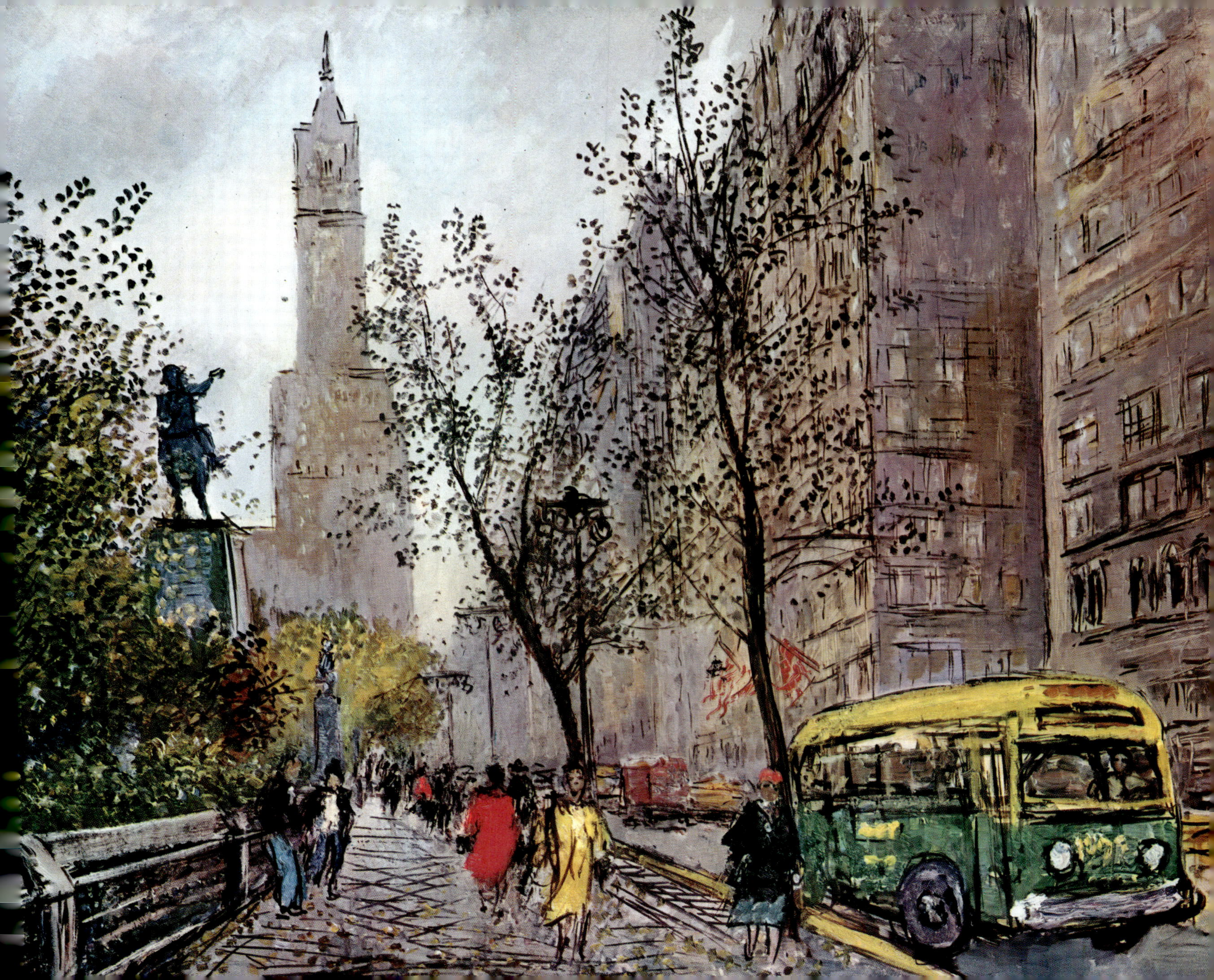

PLATE XXVIII: *Central Park South, New York*, 1961. Collection Dr. Carlo Ciulli-Ruggieri, Rome 32 x 39 ⅝ inches

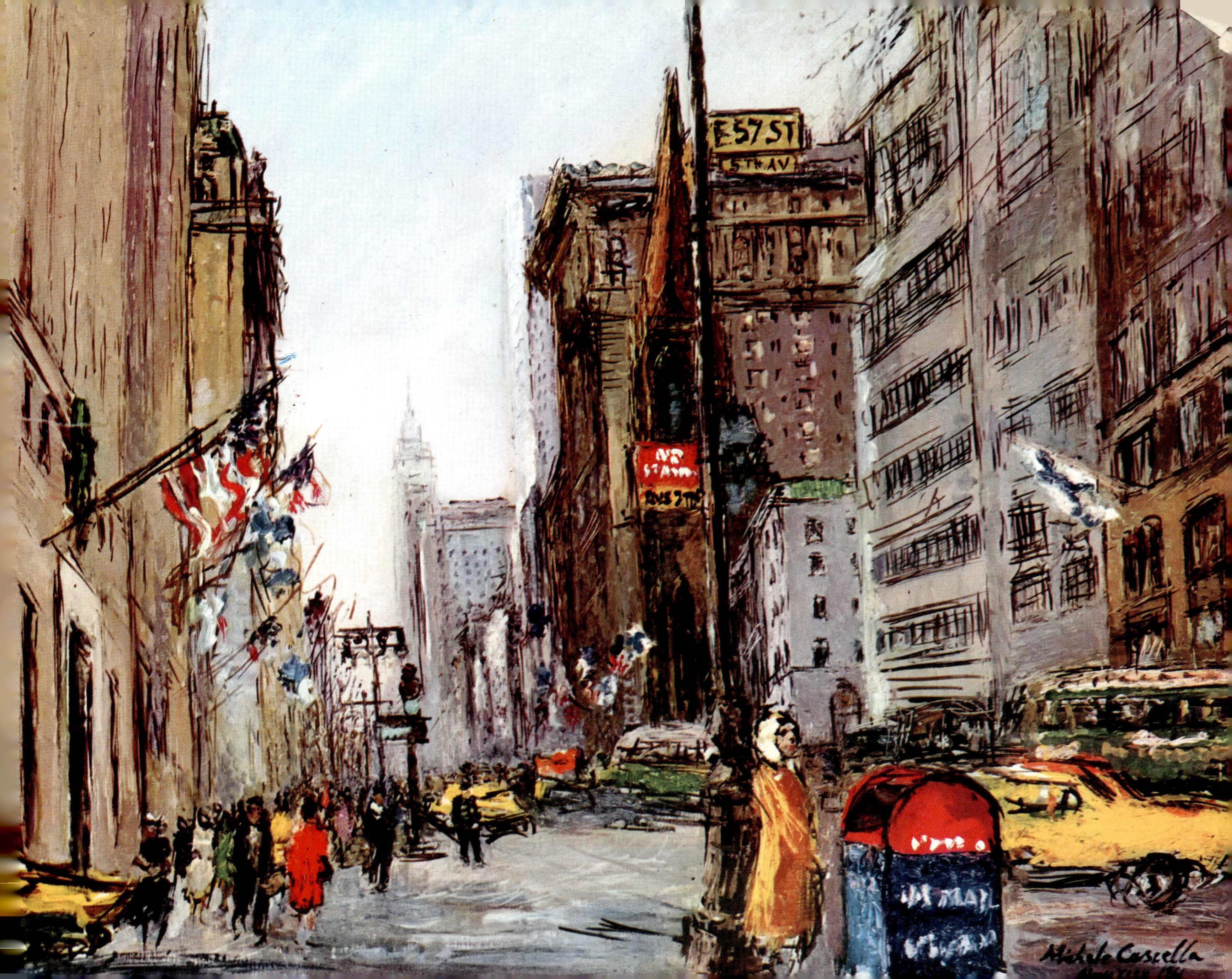
E 57 ST
5TH AV
Michele Cascella

Plate XXIX: *Fifth Avenue at 57th Street, New York*, 1961. Private Collection, Rome   32 x 39 ⅜ inches

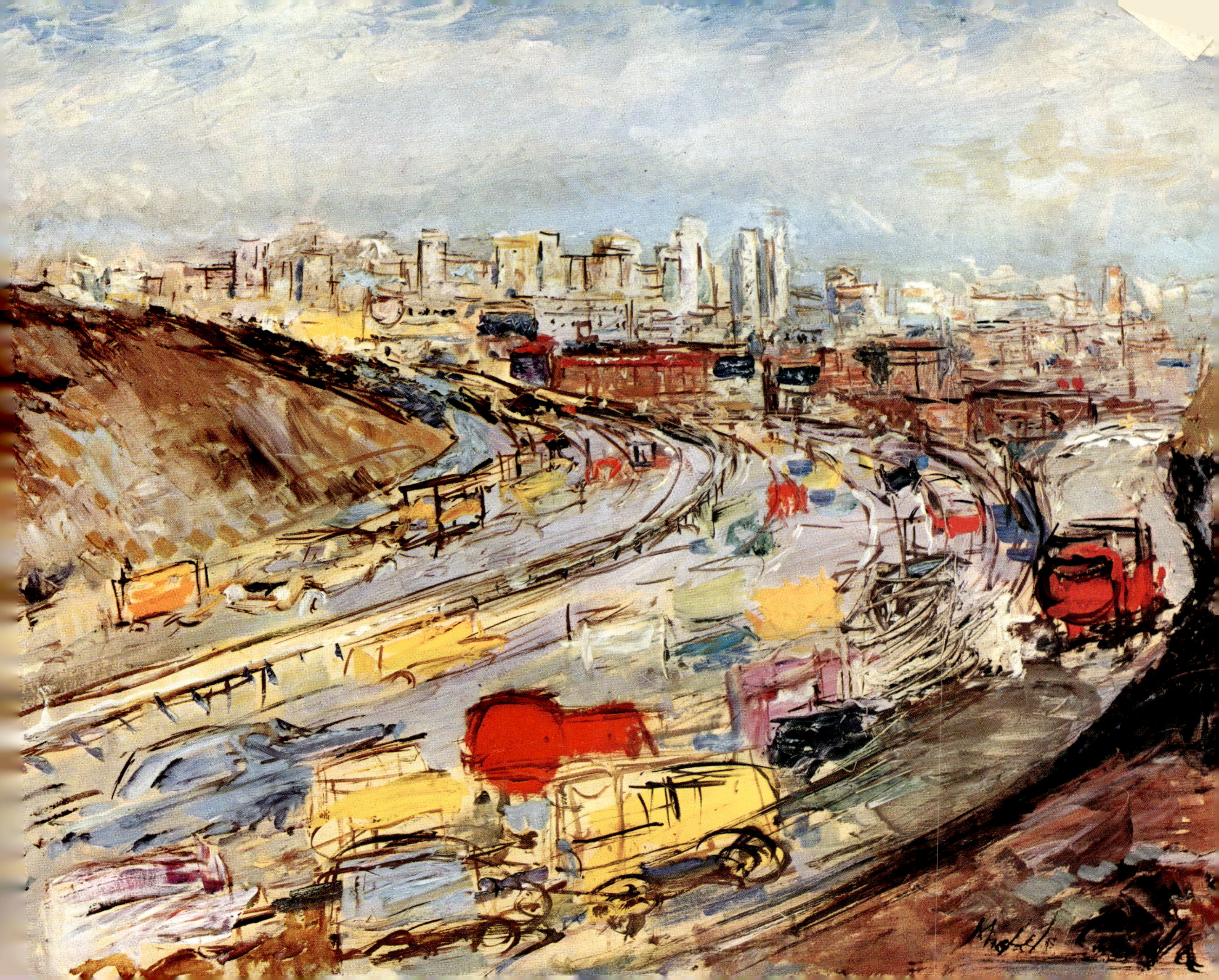

PLATE XXX: *Bayshore Freeway to San Francisco,* 1962. Private Collection, Rome   32 x 39 ⅜ inches

PLATE XXXI: *Autumn Flowers*, 1959. Collection Roberto and Zara Colombo, Turin 28 ¾ x 39 ⅜ inches

LIST OF ILLUSTRATIONS

BLACK AND WHITE

PAGE

11 *The Poetess,* 1914
12 *Fatigue Shoes,* 1915
15 *The Cathedral of Aquileia,* 1914. Collection G. Cavazzini, Parma
16 *Sailboats in Ischia,* 1915. Collection Cornelius V. Starr, New York
17 *Irises* (pastel), 1912
19 *The Red Jacket,* 1918. Collection Mrs. Liana Basedow, Rome
21 *Brother and Sister* (pastel), 1910
22 *Old Fisherman,* 1908
23 *Harvest in the Abruzzi,* 1923. Banca Nazionale del Lavoro, Rome
24 *Russian Student,* 1928
27 *Self Portrait,* 1942. Collection Dr. Delfo Palmerio, Turin
28 *Artists at Montmartre,* 1960. Collection Mr. and Mrs. Walter H. Shorenstein, San Francisco
29 *The Artist's Daughter,* 1949. Collection Cornelius V. Starr, New York
30 *The House of Keats and Shelley, Rome,* 1959. Collection Carlo Ermoli, Milan
32 *Piazza Santa Maria Novella, Florence,* 1949. Collection Museum of Modern Art, Paris
34 *The Artist's Studio,* 1958
35 *Trinitá dei Monti, Rome,* 1959. Collection Fred Zinnemann, Hollywood California
37 *Sutter Creek Bar,* 1961. Collection Mr. and Mrs. Willis A. Roller Los Altos Hills, California
38 *The Golden Gate, San Francisco,* 1960. Collection Ing. Angelo Farsura, Milan
39 *The Gold Rush,* 1961
41 *American Ballerina,* 1961. Collection Mr. Abe Ginsburg, Teaneck, New Jersey
42 *Small Market in Portofino,* 1962. Collection Dr. Pietro Gambetta, Genoa
43 *The Yellow Car.* Private Collection, Rome
44 *Monastery of Michetti, Francavilla on-the-Sea*
49 *Mrs. Sybil Forster, Menlo Park, California*
50 *Little Francesca, Palo Alto, California.* Collection Mrs. Sybil Forster, Menlo Park, California
51 *The Poet Clemente Rebora.* Collection Society of Friends of Clemente Rebora
52 *The Cathedral of Guardiagrele (Abruzzo),* 1965
52 *Piazza San Marco, Venice* (watercolor), 1964. Private Collection Beverly Hills, California
53 *The Home of Wally Toscanini, Venice* (watercolor), 1964
53 *The Harbor of Ortona (Abruzzo),* 1965
54 *Pont des Arts, Paris* (watercolor), 1964. Collection Dr. Carlo Giudici, Milan
55 *The Convent at Guardiagrele (Abruzzo),* 1965
56 *New York, Fifth Avenue (at 60th),* 1959. Collection Mrs. Marcus Rothschild, New York.
123 *The Fountain of Trevi.* Collection Miss Joyce Passetti, Menlo Park, California

COLOR PLATES

PLATE

I *White Dwellings* (pastel) 1909
II *Russian Soldiers*, 1915
III *The Artist's Mother*, 1923
IV *The River Pescara*, 1923
V *Canonization of Andrea Uberto Fournet*, 1933
VI *Capri*, 1935
VII *Flowers for Martha.* Collection André Toriel, Lausanne
VIII *Window at Portofino*, 1957. Collection Julian Silverstein, North Bergen, New Jersey
IX *Dinner Table in California*, 1960
X *Ice Skating at Central Park, New York*, 1959. Collection Miss Patricia Miller, New York
XI *Path of Lilies*, 1949. Collection Dr. Pietro Gambetta, Genoa
XII *Santa Margherita Ligure*, 1959. Collection William Glasser, San Antonio, Texas
XIII *The Arcades in Portofino*, 1960. Collection Mrs. Helena Charlton, Phoenix, Arizona
XIV *People at Portofino*, 1960. Collection Ing. Lino del Favero, Milan
XV *Piazza in Portofino*, 1960. Collection Mr. Ralph L. Dickman, Tacoma, Washington
XVI *Café Le Rouquet, Paris*, 1960. Private Collection, Venice
XVII *Obsession of New York*, 1961
XVIII *Tuileries, Paris*, 1960. Collection Dr. and Mrs. Max Kameny, Oakland California
XIX *Place Furstenberg, Paris*, 1960. Collection Marco Heidner, Tacoma Washington
XX *Parisian Autumn*, 1959. Collection Mr. and Mrs. H. Bradley Jones, Pasadena, California
XXI *Piazza d'Arquata Scrivia*, 1959. Collection Ing. Walter Comani, Pescara
XXII *New York Public Library*, 1959. Collection Sergio Bonelli, Milan
XXIII *Flowers of California*, 1961. Collection Mrs. Luisa Peretti, Rome
XXIV *The Medici Fountain, Luxembourg Gardens, Paris.* Collection Mrs. Matilde Monzino, Milan
XXV *Sixth Avenue, New York*, 1962
XXVI *The Promised Land*, 1961. Private Collection, Hamburg
XXVII *The Carmel Beach, California*, 1961
XXVIII *Central Park South, New York*, 1961. Collection Dr. Carlo Ciulli-Ruggieri, Rome
XXIX *Fifth Avenue at 57th Street, New York*, 1961. Private Collection, Rome
XXX *Bayshore Freeway to San Francisco*, 1962. Private Collection, Rome
XXXI *Autumn Flowers*, 1959. Collection Roberto and Zara Colombo, Turin

The Fountain of Trevi. Collection Miss Joyce Passetti, Menlo Park, California 16 x 20 inches

REPRODUCTIONS IN BLACK AND WHITE
AND IN COLOR, THE PRINTING AND
BINDING ARE BY STABILIMENTO D'ARTI
GRAFICHE AMILCARE PIZZI S.p.A., MILANO